Children at the Margins:
Supporting Children, Supporting Schools

Children at the Margins:
Supporting Children, Supporting Schools

edited by Tom Billington
and Michael Pomerantz

Trentham Books

Stoke on Trent, UK and Sterling, USA

Trentham Books Limited

Westview House	22883 Quicksilver Drive
734 London Road	Sterling
Oakhill	VA 20166-2012
Stoke on Trent	USA
Staffordshire	
England ST4 5NP	

First published 2004

British Library Cataloguing-in-Publication Data
A catalogue record for this book is available from the British Library

1 85856 324 0

Cover illustration: Ken Sprague

The views expressed by each of the authors in this book are personal and are not intended to reflect either the views or policies of any employer organisation.

Designed and typeset by Trentham Print Design Ltd., Chester and printed in Great Britain by Cromwell Press Ltd, Wiltshire.

Contents

Acknowledgements

We would like to dedicate this book to all the children and young people who appear in the book and who are striving to hold on to their hopes and potential, and also to the adults in their lives.

We would also like to acknowledge the involvement and support of valued colleagues and fellow professionals. Firstly Dr. David Thompson who has for many years provided a context for the development of educational psychology practice at the University of Sheffield, based on principles of mutual respect and tolerance as well as scholarly criticality.

Many other members of the Doctoral programme in educational psychology have also made significant contributions to the book, either through their own presentations or through their involvement in discussions and lively debates.

As Course Secretary, Jean Booker has provided us with valuable administrative support, and Joanne Billington devoted many hours work at the authors' proof-reading stage.

We would like to thank Ken Sprague for giving us permission to use his art work and finally we owe our thanks to Dr. Gillian Klein, Editor and other staff at Trentham Books for their vision, close reading and unwavering support for the project.

Notes on contributors

Dr. Tom Billington is Course Director for the practitioner Doctoral programme in Educational Psychology at the University of Sheffield. He also provides Expert Witness testimony to the Courts regarding the care, custody and protection of children.

Dr. Mike Pomerantz is a Senior Educational Psychologist in Derbyshire and an Associate Tutor to the post-graduate programmes in Educational Psychology at the University of Sheffield.

Dr. Tiny Arora is a Specialist Senior Educational Psychologist in Kirklees and Associate Tutor at the Educational Psychology Training and Doctoral Programme at the University of Sheffield.

Katie Clarke is the mother of six children between the ages of thirteen and five years old. She is Chair of 1 Voice – Communicating Together and works in her spare time as a Development Worker for the Calderdale Parent and Carers Council.

Daniela Mercieca is an Educational Psychologist who is working in Malta and is currently reading a Ph.D at the University of Sheffield. Her focus is on exploring the dilemmas that an Educational Psychologist faces on an everyday basis.

Dr. Richard Gamman is an Educational Psychologist currently working in Peterborough.

Jackie Lown is an Associate Tutor at the University of Sheffield and Specialist Senior Educational Psychologist at the City of York.

Dr. Stephanie James is an Associate Tutor at the University of Sheffield.

Lynne Mackey works as an Educational Psychologist in Kirklees. She is also working in a multi-agency team to help provide suitable provision for difficult to place youngsters.

Lynn Turner is a Senior Educational Psychologist in Leeds and a member of the Doctoral programme in Educational Psychology at the University of Sheffield.

Brian Willis is a Senior Educational Psychologist in Doncaster and a member of the Doctoral programme in Educational Psychology at the University of Sheffield.

Keith Venables is a Senior Educational Psychologist in Derbyshire. He is committed to inclusion and believes that education can be transformed for the better by listening to – and taking seriously – the views of children, young people, their parents and carers.

1

Resisting social exclusion

Tom Billington and Michael Pomerantz

He drew a circle that shut me out –
Heretic, rebel, a thing to flout.
But Love and I had the wit to win:
We drew a circle that took him in!
Outwitted Edwin Markham (1936)

What this book is about

The drive to improve standards in the education systems of England and Wales has occurred at the same time as anxieties have escalated about the consequences of social exclusion. Simultaneously, international guidance and UK legislation have exhorted professionals to consider both the rights of children as well as their views, for example the UN Convention on Children's Rights (Unicef, 1989) and the revised Code of Practice in Special Educational Needs (DfES, 2002).

People working in education are thus confronted on a day-to-day basis by the issues that arise from the various policy and legislative changes and there is frequently a need for professionals to be able to adjust by developing new approaches and practices. The Green Paper (subtitled *Every Child Matters*) (DfES, 2003) is a recent initiative arising out of a constellation of circumstances which have at their core anxieties about young people such as their educational achievements and their general well-being.

[Green Paper]...aims to reduce the numbers of children who experience educational failure, engage in offending or anti-social behaviour... ensure that no child falls through the net and help every child to achieve their potential... how best can young people be involved in local decision-making? (Department for Education and Skills, 2003)

Children at the Margins meanwhile had itself originally been conceived as a means of considering just those dilemmas which are simultaneously to improve achievements in schools and to reduce social exclusion but also listen to the *voice of the child*. We do not view these dilemmas as necessarily mutually exclusive or competing and in this book we offer for peer scrutiny a range of existing professional interventions based on a determination to:

- re-affirm a commitment to the value of education for all children

- inform the development of professional practices that resist rather than lead to social exclusion

- encourage professionals to develop practices that enhance the participation of all children not just in their own education but in all the decision making processes that affect their lives.

Education has traditionally tended to imbibe from psychology a simplistic and linear model of child development. For some years, however, other arguments have focused upon the complexity of this development and have even questioned the nature and concept of childhood itself, suggesting that its too rigid definition serves a largely bureaucratic function (see Aries, 1962, James, Jenks and Prout, 1998 and Burman, 1994). Such sources suggest that a host of abilities, predilections and characteristics invested in children have themselves emerged from adult and professional accounts born out of the needs and pragmatics of contemporary government.

Social constructions of childhood have thus contributed to the ways in which children have been excluded from democratic processes and have effectively, through a simplistic model, suggested that adults are competent whilst children are not. Given that adults have assumed the power to define the boundaries of childhood, we have a particular concern for the ways in which professionals construct their representations of children. For this reason we have drawn upon the *children's voices* literature generally but especially the works of Derrick Armstrong (2003), Peter Clough and Len Barton (Eds. 1998) and Michele Moore (Ed. 2000) who have all been valued colleagues at the University of Sheffield. These authors have for some years sought consistently to challenge practices which discriminate against or unthinkingly oppress children who both struggle to meet institutional demands and transgress the norms of social contexts.

We are therefore sympathetic to social constructionist accounts of psychopathologies as well as sensitive to realist notions of individual distress and we seek to raise issues at different levels of the individual, the systemic and the governmental. Throughout, however, we have searched for broadly emancipatory approaches to education, child psychology and child care generally which are based on the editors' previous work, for example, Billington, 2000, Pomerantz and Pomerantz, 2002.

Common threads underpinning much of our work have been articulated by the United Nations Convention on the Rights of the Child (1989), in particular Article 12 (which relates to accessing the views of children). In particular, we search for different arenas of practice in which full implementation of the Convention would beg major changes in the relationships between children and professionals.

The book leads us especially to consider those social processes in which the fundamental discourses and values of our society are played out in the lives of our children. We often revisit a number of fundamental issues:

- the age at which can children make decisions about their own behaviour or their own learning

- the abilities which determine whether children are allowed to participate in all the other decision making aspects of their own lives which are currently conducted by adults in a number of different social spheres such as the care system

Thus we try to locate our practical work within disputes not only about children's rights but also about their responsibilities and we provide models of intervention and practice which the reader can utilise in their own work.

It is impossible to consider all the possible forms of marginalisation, exclusion and discrimination in one book. We seek instead to challenge theories and practices which serve to marginalise the children with whom we work. Once again, it is through the examination of the social processes within our own professional domains rather than the reification of any specific categories that the authors look to achieve more progressive, ethical approaches to working with children and young people.

It is important to declare something of the origins of our project so that the reader can better understand the various positions they might detect.

Origins of a book

On a crisp October weekend in the Autumn of 2001 the group of authors who wrote this book gathered at Barmoor which is a large, rural, Quaker residential retreat nestled in the southern borders of the North Yorkshire Moors. Some of us had been there before and harboured very fond memories of shared learning and socialising in a quiet and peaceful setting with log fires and the time and space for reflection. It was a special place to meet without the usual demands to produce something tangible. We ate communally with food we had brought and everyone had a gentle mix of time with others and time to be alone.

The group consisted of educational psychologists who were all former teachers and who were either staff or doctoral candidates at the University of Sheffield. One of the booking conditions for visitors at Barmoor is that participants are supposed to be there for some spiritual or educational reason. Our reason was a passion for researching and working with young people.

It did not take long during the sessions to identify that we had some shared values and concerns coupled with a desire to expose these to a wider community. We all took something meaningful away from the weekend and communicated it to colleagues elsewhere but before we departed we realised that we wanted to write a book together which is certainly something this particular group had never done before.

We found that what repeatedly brought us together was a profound dislike for the process of marginalisation, and even scapegoating, in all its various obvious and not so obvious forms. In our work we had struggled with being asked to help others understand the problems of promoting inclusion and reducing exclusion. We felt that one of the best ways to research these processes was to find ways in our own work which would encourage both ourselves and others to listen to the voices of those who are marginalised in society, with particular reference to children and young persons. In this book we use these latter terms interchangeably. They produce the voices which often go unheard in schools and in our other institutional arenas which function as authority in children's lives.

As suggested, the range of potentially marginalised pupils is vast and we have been unable to compile a definitive list of examples but these suggestions are offered to readers. Mere membership in any of the groups cited below neither confirms nor ignores an individual voice and there are plenty of exceptions; these individuals can be vulnerable and their voices, which can be gifts to us, are certainly underrepresented.

There are those who get into trouble and who might be described as violent or challenging, as substance abusers, truants, educationally and behaviourally difficult (EBD), as bullies and some of their victims and also as racists, drug dealers and perpetrators. There are those who are depicted as having additional special educational needs (SENs), for example those described as multi-sensory impaired, physically impaired, hearing impaired, visually impaired, autistic or as having a communication difficulty or moderate or severe learning difficulty.

There are people who have been seriously socially disadvantaged in life by virtue of being in public care, through underachieving, being unforthcoming, having parents who are poor, or because of offending behaviours, mental health problems or by being abused physically, emotionally and sexually. There are those who are unwell or else who find themselves with an unwanted pregnancy, extreme dependency or a need to look after others such as young carers. There are also those at risk of exclusion by virtue of racial, ethnic, religious or cultural status. There are recognised and unrecognised refugees and asylum seekers, travellers and highly mobile pupils. There are students who feel their sexual orientation sets them apart from others. And there are those individuals who have already encountered rejection and who have in some way been excluded from the society they should inhabit. Many children within the above groups might already suffer marginalisation and are quite likely invisible to the normal community, except perhaps through non-conformity.

The terrain in this book is potentially vast since marginalisation will not only happen to individuals from these categories and there will be those who do not necessarily identify with any of the above descriptions, and who may still have become alienated in their own situation. Indeed, in several places within the book it becomes clear that it is not only the children who can experience such marginalisation but also their teachers and no doubt their psychologists.

Undoubtedly, however, there are some individual children who, by their very association with a particular category, might become more vulnerable to the effects of social disadvantage in its many forms and whose situation is not alleviated by successful professional intervention.

Either being excluded or feeling one is about to be excluded can be a horrible place to be. Feeling unheard or failing to engage meaningfully compounds the process and can make it worse. Enduring this state for months and years can create chronic feelings of helplessness. There is something deeply offensive to social justice in witnessing fellow human beings pushed out through overt or covert marginalisation, or sitting on the edge anticipating some form of social rejection. And yet the phenomenon is so widespread throughout society that we are bound to ask basic questions about the process. Is it inevitable? Is it preventable? Is there anywhere to look for clues to reduce its harmful effects? We think the best place to go looking for innovative solutions is to communicate with those who have the most to lose, rather than confining our conversations to adults who are overrepresented in terms of being heard or read. However, there are also instances in this book when listening to adults or fellow professionals has been profitable.

Nevertheless, the direction of our project is clear, addressing as we do the violation of human rights and equal opportunities. The book looks to encourage professional practices which involve young people as active participants rather than as passive objects to be studied yet again, and we are looking for signs of optimism and the visible impact of innovative ways of working.

In our collective work we can become overly familiar with the negative processes associated with voices which are not sought out, heard and comprehended. There is such waste of talent, insight and perspective when meaningful and regular consultation with vulnerable people is underused. We are talking about conversations which never take place, or if they do something fails in the way of purposeful communication; conversations might get started but they do not get finished. Morale is then lowered and energy is lost. Hopelessness lingers in anticipation and the seeds of alienation are sewn. These pupils can be tempted into self-defeating behaviour as we ourselves might be, if faced with this situation. We see their behaviour as norm violating.

The negative outcomes which follow these negative processes include the attachment of unnecessary and unhelpful labels and stigma to individual children, revealing the industry of psychopathologisation which extends far beyond our own litany of categories. In the process this marginalisation often places the blame or responsibility on the owner rather than upon the community which produces the conditions for judgement and it can arrest the diagnostic work of looking for causes by placing the burden either upon the abnormal student's individual biology or impoverished repertoire of behaviour. Whilst the process of looking for within-child factors may be economic in the short term it is also uneconomic in the long term because it leaves the host culture of the school with a diminished set of tools with which to address problems.

Systems theory tells us about homeostasis or the tendency for organisations to engage in stagnating practice that perpetuates the status quo. Some pessimists within schools do not really expect much change, feeling that all this is inevitable and has been addressed unsuccessfully for years by educational innovators and political schemes. Some hold the view that marginalisation is a perfectly natural Darwinian (survival of the fittest) social process which cannot be cured by simple social engineering by well intended and perhaps politically naïve practitioners. Some might take a moralistic position, holding that marginalisation and exclusion are in many cases appropriate consequences for those who swim upstream and behave in a manner that somehow violates what the majority believe about how to behave properly. To pursue this argument they are perhaps less concerned with real or potential violation of human rights.

This negative cycle infects our communities every time one individual is prevented from making his or her contribution. When measured, their attainments and attendance figures do not assist in making one school look attractive to others. It is these pupils being seen as the problem rather than as a part of the solution that results in schools being judged as causing concern or in need of special measures. When the situation is desperate these very pupils might just hold some of the social and curriculum answers that schools otherwise seek by paying outside expert consultants large fees. The cycle ends with lost opportunities and time lost which may go unnoticed. Best Value is not achieved. We have not made an appropriate investment in those who are marginalised. It is wasteful.

However, we have experience of alternative positive processes which is what readers will find in the pages of this book. In what follows we will hear narratives of voices heard and stories told, of pupils who are placed in situations where they are listened to or else consulted and involved in decision making in a conspicuous manner. The willingness and at times hunger to communicate and to contribute by the young people will become evident. Energy is identified, valued and harnessed to the benefit of the whole educational community.

Positive processes can naturally lead us to visible and positive outcomes as some stories will reveal. The noticeable gains include raising self-esteem, confidence, competence, attainments, autonomy, self-control, self-awareness, and increased participation. We can see more empathy, insight, sharing, attachment, engagement and commitment. Involving these young people more actively in decisions about their lives teaches real citizenship and a better understanding of rights, responsibilities and ownership. It looks at belonging, prejudice, discrimination, poverty, democracy, power, control, rights, politics, accountability, integration, inclusion and feeling valued.

When asked later in life to vote in an election the activity might seem more relevant to those who have been able to practise their democratic skills through a fuller participation within their own education.

The more positive approaches suggest we look purposefully at context for clues to account for why a pupil population within a school, for example, becomes socially stratified, with all those candidates for social exclusion being pushed to the margins of a predictable social circle which constitutes acceptability and popularity. It is a move away from the normal preoccupation with within-child factors. We look at the whole social setting which can extend beyond the walls of school to include the family and the wider community. We look to a raft of interventions like circles of friends, nurture groups, student-teacher days, multi-agency work, partnerships, teamwork, pupil forums, pupil centred research, changes to the curriculum and assessment, systems analysis, organisational restructuring, advocacy, teacher training and consultation.

Structure of the book

We start with consideration of individual young people in order to expose some of the successes and failures of professional interventions. In the middle of the book we consider a number of ways in which professionals look more actively and systematically to include young people. The final chapters provide vivid accounts of ways in which young people have provided valuable insights into their own abilities and potentials within educational settings.

In particular, the first three chapters each contain the author's representation of a single child who, through no fault of their own, has had to negotiate a number of situations in which the prime responsibility has rested with adults and professionals. It is an important theoretical principle of the book that such representations should only be considered as such and not as a professional sequestration of the truth of that individual child. Acknowledging such accounts as our own does not as a *sine qua non* invalidate the authorial voice but merely identifies a crucial theoretical point which allows us to see more clearly those analyses that lie within the orbit of professional knowledge and those that lie beyond it.

Jackie Lown cites the case of a boy called Daniel, whose fate seems largely to depend on some haphazard, often informal arrangements between a number of agencies, each of which is able to deny responsibility at crucial moments. Jackie suggests from her position as a Senior Educational Psychologist working for a Local Education Authority that the UK Government's support for unified Children's Services would seem a logical response to the systems failures which exacerbate the chaos and distress in the lives of many children.

Tom Billington likewise locates his chapter at the intersection of a child's social well-being and educational achievement. He was instructed by the Court to provide an opinion in respect of various care and custody issues. He gives us an account of a black boy, Callum, who is in grave danger of becoming marginalised due to lack of family and service support. In particular, the eliciting of Callum's own view was central in the formation of professional opinion, however inconvenient this may have been for the agencies who had to deal with the situation.

Daniela Mercieca describes her work with a boy called Adrian, whilst she was a teacher in her home country of Malta. Daniela sees the relationship she shares with Adrian as crucial to achieving a more positive outcome for him. However, she brings sharply into focus the experience of the adult professional who attempts to deal with the troubled child in a difficult situation and, therefore, to provide links to the reader's own experiences of such situations.

Whilst the first three chapters concentrate on accounts of individuals, each nevertheless suggests the need for change in professional practices. Each author exposes the responsibility of the adults, but we advise against a reductionist account of the power relationships which exist between adults and children.

In Chapter Four Stephanie James brings these power relationships into sharp focus as she considers ways in which psychologists can listen to children through the processes of professional consultation. However, in her reflexive practice Stephanie develops a series of questions which psychologists might usefully ask themselves when working ethically with children.

In the following chapter Brian Willis takes a challenging look at conventional practice in which young children are regarded as having social or emotional difficulties. In his critique of nurture groups Brian exposes the paradox that in trying to identify children who might benefit from extra support, these children can suffer marginalisation which is a threat possibly greater than any benefit to be accrued. He also reveals the ways in which age is used as a way of disallowing the views of very young children.

Keith Venables and Katie Clarke consider the actual role of Educational Psychologists in the process in which children with disabilities may either be supported or excluded. Katie, a parent of a disabled child and Keith describe some of their work together in which they search for a different position for successful professional intervention. In particular, they discuss the possibilities offered by a social as opposed to a medical model of Educational Psychology.

The last four chapters seek to provide the reader with accounts of research conducted with children in schools up and down the country. Tiny Arora and Lynne Mackey address the thorny problem of providing the right kind of support for children who are in receipt of a medicalised diagnosis of ADHD (Attention Deficit Hyperactivity Disorder). Their research considers the accounts of young people dealing with the consequences of that diagnosis.

Lynn Turner's account of the innate desire of young people both to learn and to aspire to a healthy social context has a freshness which belies the difficult school situations which participants experienced. Importantly, Lynn raises the issue that students may possess competences which the professionals could use to resurrect the fortunes of the school. Simplistic assumptions of professional competence and child incompetence are thus reversed in a radical way.

Richard Gamman exposes this possibility also, by addressing the nature not merely of pupil behaviour but of allowing the young people to inform arguments about the content of the curriculum. Gamman's challenge is also directed at different levels; the individual, systemic and the governmental, when he reveals the dissatisfaction pupils feel about their experience of a Key Stage Three English curriculum. Richard reveals a shifting emphasis from a liberal tradition of personal growth to a mechanistic acquisition of basic skills, a model reminiscent of Thomas Gradgrind in Dickens' *Hard Times*.

Finally, Michael Pomerantz describes in his chapter the potentially radical project in which he worked with teachers and young people in a high school to see whether these non-professionals would benefit educationally when given the opportunity to assume responsibility for the learning context. Should we be surprised about the ways in which the young people responded to the challenge by creating their own opportunities? We see possibilities for a different kind of partnership between education professionals and young people which could be built upon confidence and mutual respect.

Summary
Our emphasis is on adults listening more and children and young people speaking out. And while most of the examples are adult-directed, others suggest a shift in the relationships between adults and young people.

The book raises important issues which arise out of professional practice and which have ramifications for future work. The thrust of the book is directed at the hard-pressed practitioner who can identify with the situations described here.

Engaging with theoretical first principles constitutes a necessary professional activity and some readers may well develop a thirst for further study in this respect. In this case we direct the reader to texts which pose many challenges to existing practices, such as Erica Burman's *Deconstructing Developmental Psychology* (1994) and her co-authored *Psychology, Discourse Practice* (1996), as well as Wendy Hollway's *Subjectivity and Method in Psychology* (1989) and also Hollway and Jefferson's *Doing Qualitative Research Differently* (2000).

Some of the recurring themes in this book relate to issues of power and representation and in the texts above the reader can find some roots for positions taken in *Children at the Margins*. More rigorous theoretical approaches can be found in the works of Michel Foucault (for example, 1977) and Jacques Lacan (1977) (see also Billington, 1995 and 2002).

One example of the way theory and practice can become intertwined is in our approach to confidentiality. The young people in the *Belper Project* wanted their work to be identified and acknowledged. In all other cases within the book, however, we have adopted a policy of anonymity and as such all proper names have been avoided or changed.

What we share and hope to convey to you here is the conspicuously strong social justice agenda which underlies our project. We seek to resist practices which can be unnecessarily oppressive and restrictive by searching for other kinds of professional action to support the vital changes which must take place if all schools are to be improved in line with social expectations.

There is new material here which can be reflected upon, applied in local situations, given a willingness to experiment with a vision that in difficult circumstances, school life can improve. Perhaps the place to start is with local evidence-based research. See if there is anything in the pages that follow that is worthwhile testing out for yourselves and see if it works.

We would like to commend the ordinariness of the situations we describe, which are commonplace and familiar to many professionals working with children. Whilst the situations may be ordinary, however, the children with whom we work are not. In the course of the book we will expose and resist the inherently alienating processes within our contemporary cultural contexts, which are so corrosive of hope and justice.

Undoubtedly, we are at a place in history in which many of the institutional contexts and models of professional authority which have been constructed over the last three hundred years are being challenged. Currently, however, any attempts to resist the social exclusion and marginalisation of children in general and children with 'special' difficulties in particular, have been thwarted.

In *Children at the Margins* we aim to support and revitalise the work of those professionals who work with children and who are endeavouring to challenge those practices and forms of organisation which oppress many of our children.

2

Children in need of services and in public care: Opening up systems for effective joint working

Jackie Lown

This chapter will:

- consider the benefits to children of Local Authorities delivering fully joined up services

- explore why Local Authorities encounter difficulties in providing efficient and effective joined up solutions to address educational disadvantage

- use open systems theory as a framework to argue that organisations cannot maximise the potential of joined up working unless they share the same primary task and share the same internal organisational culture

- use a case study, *Daniel*, to illustrate how open systems theory can be used to explore decision making processes within a Local Authority. Professionals purporting to work together for the same end – to improve Daniel's life chances – readily lose sight of his wishes. The decision to marginalise him from family, school and community is legitimised by professionals and parents.

Case Study

Daniel (based on a real case, but names have been changed) had a Statement of Special Educational Needs from the age of six, recognising Emotional and Behavioural Difficulties (EBD). School staff contacted social services several times due to worries about Daniel's reported behaviour outside school; there was already involvement with the family due to his older sister. The response was that in the parents' view, Daniel was not a worry to them. Consequently no further action was taken, though a social worker continued to be in contact with the family. School staff felt very frustrated that "nothing was being done" by social services. Following a temporary exclusion, Daniel was put on a part time re-integration programme and a referral was made to a clinical psychologist.

In the period when Daniel was attending school part time, the Education Social Worker (ESW), together with police officer on *truancy watch*, picked Daniel up twice in town, during the afternoons when he was not in school. The ESW was concerned about Daniel's well-being, having seen him being chastised by parents and locked in a shed for a small misdemeanour. She reported this to social services.

A review of Daniel's Statement of Special Educational Needs (SEN) in Year 5 involved his parents, clinical psychologist, educational psychologist, teacher in charge of the unit, head teacher and social worker. School staff made it clear that residential placement would be best for Daniel. In private conversation with me, the teacher in charge described this as a way to remove him from the home situation, felt to be the cause of the growing difficulties. The social worker said this might be the best solution, but reiterated that his parents had not regarded Daniel as a real problem. An older sister was their main difficulty. It was pointed out that a residential school would usually only be considered when there was a clear history of services having worked closely together to provide joined up support. The clinical psychologist assessed Daniel as having attachment problems, and suggested that separation from his mum might be the only way to help repair this relationship difficulty. His mum said that she was sure that letting her son go to a residential school was best and that she would always blame herself if he was denied this chance.

The request for residential school placement was consequently raised at a multi-agency managers' meeting, involving senior managers from social services, education, housing and health services. The outcome was a directive to case workers to pull together to devise a package of support to prevent the need for residential placement. At a meeting of the caseworkers, foster placement was suggested to establish whether the alleviation of family pressures might allow some improvement in Daniel's ability to cope in school, whilst admittedly raising other pressures. The social worker explained that foster placement would only be sought when the need was established through intensive casework and family assessment. She described Daniel's difficulties as educational, unrelated to family circumstances. The question of resource allocation and priorities was high on the agenda, though unacknowledged.

Daniel then began to receive home tuition, which put increasing pressure on the family; increasingly parents saw residential school as the only solution. Consequently, temporary foster placement now became even less likely, since potential carers would avoid taking on a child at home full time.

When discussed again at the multi-agency managers' meeting, the situation was viewed as untenable; local schooling was seen as out of the question and residential schooling seen as the only solution. Detailed discussion ensued about whether Daniel's difficulties were educational or social in nature. Although not stated, the question of which agency's budget would fund the placement was a significant factor.

Introduction

Since coming to power the government has urged public and voluntary services to move towards providing joined up solutions to address the problems of society. Encouragement has gone hand in hand with changes in the law, directive, guidance and recommendation. Joined up thinking is a term which has become part of the language of public sector working at all levels.

Hertfordshire was one of the first councils to take the step of combining aspects of education and social services in a move towards truly joined up working. This was achieved by taking the decision to 'drop its education directorate in favour of an umbrella children, schools and families directorate' (TES, 2000). Others have followed suit. The arguments for working in this way are rational and convincing.

Following Lord Laming's inquiry into the death of Victoria Climbie, September 2003 saw the publication of the Green Paper: *Every Child Matters* (DfES, 2003), carrying recommendations to reform children's care. Key proposals in the Green Paper include:

- improving information sharing between agencies

- bringing together professionals to make them more accessible to children and families

- removing organisational boundaries, professional and cultural barriers

- creating lead professionals to coordinate service provision between services

- appointment of a Director of Children's Services in all local authorities, accountable for education and social services

- in the longer term, integration of key services as part of a *Children's Trust* model, with a single planning and commissioning function and pooled budgets

- the creation at national level of a Minister for Children, Young People and Families

Definition of terms

It is important to define the term Children's Services and to outline working definitions of terms used repeatedly in this chapter. The term Children's Services is intended to denote the part of any local authority social services department (SSD) which covers services to children for whom the authority is responsible or involved in supporting in any way. Children's Services assume different names in different local authorities.

Children and young people in public care, also known as looked after children, are those children and young people for whom a local authority has corporate responsibility. The points made in this chapter apply equally to those children who have not reached the point of entering care, but are deemed as children in need of services.

Why promote joined up working practices?

Professionals are being exhorted to work together across disciplinary and institutional boundaries to develop professional practices that prevent the worst kinds of miscommunications and misunderstandings. That this is a 'good thing' is a difficult concept to challenge but developing such working practices on a day-to-day basis is notoriously difficult. (Billington and Warner, 2003 p 5)

It has been recognised for some time that successful outcomes for children and young people in the care system depend upon close collaborative working between all the adults involved in their lives. Depressing facts about the likely outcomes for these children have been reported repeatedly:

- 75% of care leavers leave formal education with no qualifications (DfEE/DoH, 2000)

- 12–19% of care leavers move on to further education, compared with 68% of the general population (Biehal *et al*, 1995)

- 12% of children in the care system are either not attending school regularly or are excluded; the figure rises to 25% for 14-16 year olds (First Key, 1999)

- Compared to national exclusion figures in 1995/6, looked after children were ten times more likely to be permanently excluded (First Key, 1999)

- 61% of offenders under the age of 21 have been in care (First Key, 1999)

Figures consistent with those listed have been repeated in several research studies such as The Audit Commission (1994). The evidence demonstrates a worrying problem inherent in the way that Local Authorities are organised to address the needs of its most vulnerable children and young people.

Many have reiterated that joined-up working practices must be improved to change the undeniable problems which have prevailed in terms of education, health and social welfare services to vulnerable children in society (Law *et al*, 2001; Normington and Kyriacou, 1994; Webb and Vulliamy, 2001). Practices must improve so that better and more effective decisions for individual children become the norm and to further promote the life chances of every child and young person entering the care system.

A further reason for strengthening multi-agency services for the benefit of vulnerable children lies in the government's commitment to the social inclusion agenda, a view shared, it seems, by many local authorities, groups and individuals (Social Exclusion Unit, 1998, 1999). The admirable, humanitarian principle of creating a society in which all individuals are, and feel they are, included is supported by political, social and economic reasons for taking such action:

- Individuals who are fully engaged in society are more likely to make an economic contribution through their own employment, and as consumers

- Such individuals are more likely to become effective parents to future children of society, and make a more positive contribution to society as adults

Truly joined up practice

Clear principles of inter-agency collaboration were being emphatically stated as far back as 1991 (Utting, 1991), with many re-statements in the years following, eg:

> The key aim of this guidance is to help to promote effective working partnerships between education and social services agencies to ensure that the children's needs are met. (SSI/Ofsted Report, 1995)

> A successful intervention cannot be achieved without a truly corporate effort – political ownership and leadership from senior management are essential. (DfEE/DoH, 2000 p 8)

Even so, only very slow progress has been apparent. If the message from the early 1990s onwards had been heard and acted upon there would be little need for the current re-statement of these principles in the Green Paper (DfES, 2003). This raises an interesting question about what has prevented such practices from being developed. Why is it, after so many years of being exhorted to work collaboratively, local authority services have not managed to be effective in meeting the educational, social and health needs of the children in its care? Open systems theory offers a useful perspective with which to explore this conundrum.

Open Systems Theory

My window on the world provides the one correct perspective from which to observe and understand reality; yours is distorted. (Miller, E. J., 1976, p 1)

Miller and Rice (1967) conceptualise organisations as 'tools designed primarily for task performance', which exist in the context of constraints brought about by environment and human needs. A distinction is made between task and human need, resulting in descriptors of *formal* and *informal* organisation respectively. The authors state,

A problem in any enterprise is the relative strengths of the formal and informal systems and the discrepancies between them. When formal and informal systems are in opposition to each other, task performance inevitably suffers. (Miller and Rice, 1967, p 5)

Miller and Rice (1967) describe organisations as systems which set out to perform a primary task; they argue that this model would apply equally to a production facility or service organisation. So, the task of a plastics factory is to manufacture a range of plastic products, whereas the task of an education department could be described as one of educating children and adults in a range of subjects and the task of a social services department could be described in terms of ensuring the social welfare of various client groups.

A further element in the open systems model concerns intakes and outputs; organisations, or systems, take in certain materials (which may, in terms of a school, be children), take the intakes through a conversion process (deliver lessons to children, which they learn from) and then make outputs (children who have learned), which makes space for new inputs/intakes to enter the system and be converted.

Regardless of the type of system certain forces will be in operation which impact upon the efficiency of the organisation and on the human needs of those within the system. One such force is regulation:

> What distinguishes a system from an aggregate of activities and preserves its boundary is the existence of regulation. Regulation relates activities to throughput, ordering them in such a way as to ensure that the process is accomplished and that the different import-conversion-export processes of the system as a whole are related to the environment. (Miller and Rice, 1967, p 8)

Two types of regulatory activity are identified: monitoring and boundary control. The monitoring aspect is the element of checking that the system is doing what it should: that the plastic products are being made properly, or that a local education authority is monitoring its performance indicators ready for an Ofsted visit. The second aspect, boundary control, has direct relevance to the remit of this chapter. This concerns:

- the way in which a system regulates its boundaries

- the way in which a system relates its activities to the environment at the boundary points

- the manner in which a system controls the import and export transactions across these boundary points

The group or organisation to which the individual has a sense of identity, commitment and belonging is described as the sentient system or sentient group and each sentient system or group has a sentient boundary. As such they have to have:

> ...methods of communication between themselves and with the external environment about their task in so far as they develop attitudes towards and beliefs about each other and about the group that transcend the purpose for which they have met... these assumptions, together with their attitudes towards their purpose, provide the emotional climate in which they meet. (Miller and Rice, 1967, p 18)

The link with local authorities starts to emerge. The tasks of education and social services are different, as described, and each has its own inputs, facilitates particular conversion processes and makes specific outputs. Within these systems, sub-systems exist (eg schools within education, children's homes within social services), which mean that the distance, in systems terms, between a school and a children's home is potentially large, since each system and sub-system has its own primary task and sub-culture which creates a *membrane* that needs to be traversed. The boundaries of the systems are set, in part, by the definition of the task and role of each organisation; Miller and Rice describe the possibility of boundary skirmishing at points of overlap.

In terms of this chapter, boundaries are traversed in matters such as education in relation to children and young people in need of services. Daniel's case conference brought together representatives from several systems and sub-systems (school, local education authority, social services, health service) in the hope that a coordinated temporary sub-system could go through an intake, conversion and output process to make improvements.

Miller and Rice describe the potential difficulties which can arise when people engage in this temporary boundary crossing; individuals take with them loyalties, cultural and organisational meanings from their own system (the sentient system) and therefore they can only be visitors to another system.

The systems theory approach, therefore, suggests that:

- There are problems inherent in the process of attempting to effectively coordinate different systems in providing shared solutions to tasks, not least because of the regulatory activities and sentient boundaries which exist within each system

- If systems share the same primary task, the possibility arises of amalgamating those systems into one new system which shares the same primary task in order to improve efficiency/ effectiveness and better satisfy the human needs of those who feel part of the sentient group

Additionally, other systems which exist outside the local authority (eg health authorities, health trusts, voluntary agencies) overlap with the local authority at several boundary points, though the areas of overlap emerge from each separate and individual system. Consequently, there are areas of focus (eg services to children) which arrive at the point of child and family from several different systems with the hope that these are coherent at the point of receipt. There exists, then, a multi-faceted set of systems, each with its own identity, orientation, sentient boundaries, culture, policies and practice; these are delivered to consumers, who cannot be expected to understand the reasons for such lack of coordination. Whether it is viable to coordinate many different departments in an efficient and effective way is questionable. The Green Paper (DfES, 2003) suggests it will be possible to create universal services sharing the same view of purpose, mission and practice.

Open Systems Theory: implications for multi-agency working

The case of Daniel illustrates the boundary skirmishing to which Miller and Rice (1967) refer. Here, the task and role boundaries defined by each organisation are being challenged by other outsider organisations, with the suggestion of further entrenchment of the behaviour which signifies who is responsible for setting out those boundaries.

Regulatory boundary control, with the accompanying implications for role definition, can often be recognised as the root cause of boundary skirmishes between Local Authority sub-systems. An example of such boundary skirmishing can be seen when professionals believe they know what another's role should be, raising irritation and questions about why these expectations are not being met. Boundary skirmishing may result from:

- **Organisational culture**: Any organisation develops, or is initially assigned, a perception of its own task, in terms of inputs, conversions and outputs. This is completely embedded within theoretical frameworks and practice which underpin the activity and are shared by those who work within the system (eg at a simple level, The Children Act has been absorbed as part of social services organisation and structure and has become an integral part of the role definition of social workers). It is very difficult for professionals from other organisations to traverse this invisible membrane as anything but a temporary visitor to it. A mainstream school teacher, for example, could have a working knowledge of The Children Act, but it is unlikely that this will have a fundamental effect on his or her teaching role. It is inevitable that, to varying degrees, professionals from one organisation will lack understanding of others' role definition, task orientation and accompanying constraints

- **Language as a barrier**: At the level of inter-departmental and inter-professional interaction, the language of each professional group can erect barriers to multi-agency working, by appearing inaccessible to others. For example, the training and experience of social workers result in language codes, styles and idioms which would be unfamiliar to most educationalists, and vice-versa. The legislation, custom and practice related to each discipline underpins this difference. Many social workers would not be aware of the DfES Code of Practice (2001) relating to special educational needs, and many educationalists would be unaware of the sections of the Children Act which drive the day-to-day practice of social workers

- **Budgets**: Local Authorities are being urged to work effectively and efficiently together (ie traverse sentient boundaries, share congruent perceptions of task) when, simultaneously, budgetary pressures can pull in completely different directions. Funds for supporting children in need are often accessed via discrete budgets belonging to social services, health and education, thereby encouraging avoidance in making provision, or resulting in squabbles about who pays the bill. Some authorities have attempted to address this issue by setting up systems to consider funding jointly (education, health and Social Services) when a child is deemed to need specialist residential placement. Budgetary consideration was a factor in determining whether Daniel's difficulties were categorised as educational or social: ie who would pay the bill for expensive support or residential placement

- **Territorial protection**: When local authorities perceive themselves as under threat, it is not surprising that the various departments want to retain a perception that the role and function of some workers are different and distinct from others. In such circumstances, clear identity can be seen as very important, keeping the role and culture of the system fully independent from others, and the boundary membrane strong; this could be perceived as critical to the very survival of the organisation, system or sub-system

- **Inconsistency and tension in the duties and policies of different aspects of local authorities**: Exclusion of a child from school is a good example of this. Corporate responsibility for a child in public care is shared between the staff of the local authority, social workers, school teachers and support staff, and as such, all should act in a way which ensures the child's best interests are met. It is difficult to see exclusion as a means of addressing the needs of a looked after child (Brodie, 2000), and yet we know that this group are greatly over-represented in exclusion figures (First Key, 1999). Daniel was no exception; unit staff felt that exclusion would indicate the severity of Daniel's need more clearly to social services, while the social worker saw it as evidence that Daniel's difficulties were primarily about schooling

In these times of inclusion (social and educational), educationalists need to be mindful of the link between emotional and behavioural difficulties and children in need and in public care. Assessments carried out by a number of professionals may contribute to a decision making process leading towards potentially segregated provision such as Statementing. It is not being suggested here that such children should never go to specialist provision, rather that the process of assessment should not confuse the absence of effective, integrated local provision (care setting or school) with the need to receive education in a residential setting.

Systems theory, as discussed, indicates that the very nature of Local Authority systems militates against fully effective, integrated services for vulnerable children and those in public care. The recommendations contained within the Green Paper recognise that the time has come to end the rhetoric and take action to move Local Authority services towards working together in a more effective, efficient and coordinated fashion. However, systems theory ideals may be threatening, confusing, frightening, stressful and disorienting for professionals to deal with. The outcomes for young people such as Daniel will hopefully make the rocky road worthy of travel. Some of the first steps on this journey might be:

- raising awareness about the vulnerability of children in need of services and looked after children amongst elected members, governors and others with a similar monitoring/ strategic brief

- raising awareness for caseworkers about the responsibilities of different professionals in relation to vulnerable children eg teachers, head teachers, governors, special educational needs co-ordinators, social workers, residential social workers, designated teachers, health personnel

- acknowledging the potential difficulties concerning issues of power, control, trust etc which are inherent in any working relationship. These issues stand not only for working relationships between professionals and parents and carers, but also between professionals (Coulling, 2000)

- establishing robust and effective procedural links between children's services and education support services (eg Educational Psychology Services, Support Teaching Services, Pupil Referral Units)

- encouraging direct and active involvement and contribution by all services to documents such as Local Authority Education Development Plans, Behaviour Support Plans, Children's Service Plans, Quality Protects Action Plans and exclusions guidelines. It is not enough for the different agencies to pay lip-service to making contributions to such documents by stating they have been consulted, or simply offering comments upon documents circulated for comment by the authoring agency

- making a multi-agency audit of previous outcomes (educational, care and health) for children looked after by the local authority, and those deemed in need of services

- ensuring effective dissemination of information and responsibilities to schools, ie to all staff

- ensuring every school has a designated teacher who is fully aware of the responsibilities of the role and is active and proactive in meeting those responsibilities

- gathering accurate Local Authority data regarding performance measures (exclusions, attendance, examination results etc) which are monitored and considered by multi-agency representatives, with appropriate action planning

• developing joint agency protocols, and encouraging joint agency debates about funding

Conclusion

The future of local authorities may be in the balance, given developments over recent years in terms of reducing role and responsibilities. The future of local authorities may depend on them becoming better able to deliver more effective, efficient and coordinated services. The Green Paper sets out the intention that Local Authorities will deliver services in a much more coordinated way, grouping functions in a manner which combines the task orientation of sub-groups.

Fully coordinated, effective, multi-disciplinary services for children may best be achieved by reconstituting the respective constituent multi-agency parts into new hybrid children's services; the objective will have been achieved if such integrated services, as one service, can truly engage in the think, plan, do, review cycle to the benefit of the children (and families) being served. Most importantly, such a service would have at its heart a shared perception of primary task, with jointly owned aims and ambitions for all the professionals involved. This is not simply a matter of housing the various agencies, with their workers, in shared buildings, appointing a joint director and re-naming them. It requires long term investment into changes in organisational culture; it will take time for a newly formed, fledgling combined service to evolve into an organisation which is unified, where all workers share the same perceptions of primary task, boundaries, culture and loyalty.

Hertfordshire's lead could be taken and furthered. Combining educational and social services with health services, creating a new service which shares the same primary task and expressed aim of furthering the social, physical and psychological welfare of children is suggested by the Green Paper. Such a system would provide services to children and their families which are integrated at the points of delivery and receipt, thus providing truly joined up thinking and joined up practice. The challenge will be to make the process more than just a paper exercise.

Postscript

In the summer of 2003, I visited Daniel in the residential school he had been attending since January. It was time for the Annual Review of the Statement of Special Educational Needs. Staff from the new school commented upon how well Daniel had settled in to the school and how much progress he had made academically since arrival. The comments of the residential school staff and the parents were consistent in condemning the Local Education Authority for not making the decision to send him to residential school sooner. Academic progress was regarded as the proof that residential placement was right for him. His parents said they were really pleased with the progress Daniel had made at school; they also commented that behaviour problems persisted during fortnightly weekend visits home. They wondered if it might be better for Daniel to come home once a month instead. As for Daniel, he only had one point to contribute to the meeting: he said emphatically that he just wished he could go home.

3
Narratives at the boundaries of care, education and the law: re-presenting Callum

Tom Billington

Introduction

Callum was (and is still) the subject of a bitter custodial dispute and long lasting child protection concerns. He attended school only occasionally during years 4 and 5 and had poor basic skills. This chapter focuses upon the simple interventions which, over the period of two years, led eventually to excellent school attendance on his part and much improved educational attainments.

In particular, this brief story chronicles the sensitive work of a learning mentor and illustrates the potential of the child care system to prioritise educational matters as a means of resisting likely long-term social exclusion. This author was involved as a psychologist providing an assessment of Callum for the High Court (Family Division) and contends that allowing Callum to articulate his wishes and making these wishes the cornerstone of professional opinion were both crucial in minimising the risks of further social exclusion.

Margins

Callum's life has been spent on the margins, literally. He was born there and despite changing circumstances, that's where he remains, a black boy in an otherwise largely white community.

He has lived most of his twelve years on a deprived post-second world war estate on the edge of a large northern city. Originally built as a post-war escape from the tenements, the estate had not at first been deprived but had represented a new start for families with new jobs. While it had been on the edge of the city it had not been on the margins but rather the place to be, a place in which thousands of people would build bright futures.

Following twenty years or so in which those lives were indeed better in a material sense, the next twenty to thirty years were marked by a painful decline in which the industries and the jobs ebbed away. There had been new jobs but they were never numerous and as soon as the penalty periods elapsed, the businesses tended to disappear, taking their government subsidies with them.

For ten years or so the community slowly died as those that could left. The sense of loss exuded by those who stayed was only exceeded by the sores of dereliction, crime and drugs. I am reminded of Achebe's *Things Fall Apart* (1988), which depicts the decline and ruin of a complete African civilisation.

This then was the decaying community into which Callum was born. Sometimes he lives there still with his volatile and vulnerable mother and younger half-sister Kylie. Their poverty is brought sharply into focus by the new money and affluence to be seen in the smart developments all around the estate.

Sometimes Callum goes to live with his father, his step-mother and her own four young children. Callum's father, Mr. Danang escaped several years ago from the decay that existed at the edge of the city, only to find himself in the decay that still exists within it. He moved from one area of the city to another but only from one margin to another. He lives, not in the centre itself which is now chic and fashionable, but just outside in that inner rim that encircles the heart of many big cities; a danger zone that has to be crossed before arriving at the tree-lined avenues and safe suburban semis.

Of course, such scenes of city life and cycles of degeneration and regeneration are not new and may belong more to sociology than to psychology. Worryingly, however, whilst these conditions are still widespread, they are no longer addressed as hard, distinct political alternatives and choices about solutions for us to make. Have we been seduced into viewing the social divisions within our society as inevitable? In concentrating only on the psychopathology of individual lives psychology sometimes suggests that such social inequalities are either invisible or irrelevant.

I suggest that some kind of political discourse is still necessary not only as a way of explaining the concept of margins as a political and economic circumstance into which an individual can be born but as a way of challenging the subsequent and sometimes consequent reduction of children's lives to a mere psychology. In this chapter, therefore, as throughout the book, margins is a social construct, a template upon which people experience their lives.

Intentionally, I have opened with a rather desolate, depressing and apparently deterministic picture of the hopelessness experienced by many in our society, from childhood onwards. Of course, lives are neither so neatly nor patronisingly to be categorised and we all know anyway that happiness does not equate with money, although I am sure that Callum and his parents would have liked the opportunity to be able to test out this hypothesis. Margins in this chapter, however, does have an explicit dimension of poverty, both material and cultural (Bourdieu, 1984), as a pervasive context for those who are born into it.

Background

For well over a year Callum chose not to attend his primary school. Any other decision would have been too dangerous. Had he gone into school he might have been physically attacked by his peers. He might also have been attacked by the general rhetoric of school life which was one of normalcy; all those of us who work with children must in some way subscribe to this concept. Callum was not normal because he had not had normal life experiences.

Had he gone into school, it might have been impossible for Callum not to have joined in the attack upon himself – for coming from the family he did. The fact that he could not read compounded his sense of shame (Laing, 1961). How do I know that he felt shame? Well, experience, personal and professional would support such a hypothesis, as would the manner of his retreat from the world, his staying at home, not speaking and trying to shrink his tall, eleven year-old frame into a smaller space. Each of these were signs that Callum did not feel able to act with confidence in the world at large, perceiving himself as less than in comparison with others of whom he was all too acutely aware.

It is important to reflect upon other theoretical first principles as a foundation for the psychologised narrative here. I am tempted by the concept of emotional literacy, not of the anodyne variety frequently espoused during recent years but rather in its authentic form (gestalt psychotherapy and transactional analysis deal with this more ruggedly: Steiner, 1984). It is possible to explain Callum's sense of shame based on understandings of transference (Klein, 1952) and counter-transference (Klein, 1957).

Whatever the theoretical preference, any psychologist has to remain aware of their own experiential responses if they are to have any hope of ever understanding the life or situation of another. However, Callum's social background was and is all too familiar. Mrs. Danang, Callum's mother, was a woman existing at the edge of a notorious family. References to the family as gangsters might suggest sharp suits, villas and sleek cars but there was not that much money to be made in this area of burnt-out cars and boarded-up buildings, dangerous rat-runs and dirty syringes. Often, there were old scores to settle and new alliances to make on the streets and in the school.

Callum was another of the many children whom I meet who cower at the prospect of a man entering the home; one of those many children who know all too well that, as night follows day, the man will deposit his own fury on to their mother in endless, mind-emptying beatings. It was, therefore too dangerous for Callum to go into school since he needed above all to stay at home and know whether his mother was safe.

The Court had asked me to assess Callum. For some time attention had been focused on his younger sister Jade, who was suffering from distressing symptoms thought to be due to sexual abuse. The perpetrator was not known and although her mother blamed her father, it was Mrs. Danang who was the one seen by the agencies as unable to protect her daughter. The couple had long been separated but Jade had become another successful statistic (ie a child removed from the care of the local authority into an adoptive placement).

So attention could now be turned to Callum. The instructions asked for my opinion as to where Callum should live since he was now the centre of a bitter parental custody dispute. Mrs. Danang said that her son was being abused by his father during visits to his home and she wanted him to be with her. Mr. Danang wanted Callum too, counter-alleging that he was being neglected by his mother and was un-protected from the violence within her home.

Callum himself was quiet, reluctant to speak to the point of with-drawal, and a target in school for bullies. He was easy prey to angry boys who greedily circulated in graphic terms the street view of his alleged sexual preferences and practices.

One recurring theme in this book, as indeed in much of my own work elsewhere (Lloyd Bennett and Billington, eds 2001, Billington and Warner, eds 2003), is the difficulty of working across professional boundaries. This is not to propose an argument for destroying those boundaries but more to find better ways of crossing them which Jackie Lown describes in the previous chapter.

The background to Court instructions about Callum concerned serious issues of safety and child protection around the home. How-ever, there was no reference to issues of his schooling and education in the Court papers, only to care. Given previous experience as a local authority Educational Psychologist (EP) as well as my own research (see also Billington, 2000, 2003), it has been impossible to avoid conclusions about the connectedness of home and school. Clearly, this is no new theory but if it is so well known to us, why do we con-tinue to organise services in such a way as both to deny the connec-tion and also further to expose the fissure?

Home and school have provided the two basic social contexts in which children have grown up in the UK for over one hundred years now and many children have no other significant institutional context within which they can negotiate their sense of identity in the world. Cognisant of this link and especially of the importance of peer relationships in school during and following family crisis and break-down, I chose firstly, therefore, to go into Callum's school and speak to his teachers.

Jenny

What I found last year in Callum's Primary School was, as usual, not all that I would have expected. Firstly, there was an activity and a bustle that breathed new life into my own sense of hope. Where did all this energy and sense of purpose come from? More than this, I was then told that during the previous few months Callum had started to attend school again. Almost unbelievably he had also at last started to read fluently and had achieved mainly level 4s in his Year Six standard assessment tests (SATs). What had happened?

The school was clearly still surrounded by social deprivation and it thus received special funds from various central and local government projects to provide for a number of extra resources. One such resource was the introduction of learning mentors; Callum had been allocated to Jenny.

When I met Jenny, she told me that she had not actually worked with Callum and so naturally I was curious about how the situation had been transformed in school. She said that initially she had simply set up a system which made it more likely that he came to school through persistent daily monitoring of his attendance. At times Callum and his mother were involved more directly when he was brought into school with a number of other children. Callum, however, was evidently now finding his way to school of his own volition and on a daily basis.

Jenny was clearly aware of the many issues surrounding Callum and his family, both in the community and in school, and she was therefore very careful to avoid placing him under too much pressure to work with her individually. Indeed, she let him know just that she was there if he ever wanted to talk and invited him to work quietly in her room with others if he needed.

Callum did not make use of such opportunities for several months and indeed it was some weeks before he would even acknowledge Jenny on the school corridor, let alone visit her room. In the meantime she had arranged a number of carefully judged interventions, which included extra support for his reading. She was especially careful to ensure that the circumstances in which this occurred did not expose him to the taunts or worse of some peers.

Gradually, Jenny noticed Callum responding to her occasional invitations to work in her room and by the time I arrived on the scene he was clearly comfortable there, even producing delicate embroideries. This had not been Jenny's idea but a consequence of leaving around a number of activities available to children should they wish.

Jenny had somehow and almost single handedly resisted one of the most fundamental exclusions that a child can suffer and had engineered the conditions in which Callum could enjoy a successful, if yet somewhat fragile rehabilitation into school life. However, the chaotic nature of his home life continued to pose a threat to this embryonic sense of security and stability.

On making initial contact with Callum's mother, I had been greeted with a volley of verbal abuse and expletives which I quickly realised had little to do with me. After a little while I became 'Tom' to her and was invited into her house. Callum presented to me there as a watchful and wary boy who had clearly been told to attend for my inspection. I let him go after a brief exchange and he ran out of the house and down the street. During that brief minute of contact I asked him whether he would see me in school with Jenny and he indicated that he would.

Once in school, Callum entered the quiet of Jenny's room and I tried to be sensitive to what must have been a changed dynamic for him for this room had acquired for him the quality of a sanctuary and it was clearly his territory. He was almost at the point of refusing to work with me as he struggled to understand the changed rules, since this was not a place of coercion but of choice.

Nevertheless, with Jenny's assistance, Callum managed to listen politely to my explanations of why I was seeing him and eventually he read for me and showed me both his work and his intelligence. By the end of the meeting he had begun to look less afraid and he agreed to see me again, first at his father's home and later, after the school holidays, on his own at a Family Centre.

The first phase of the assessment had been crucial. Clearly, Callum had been clawed back from beyond the realms of the margins through Jenny's hard work, in particular by the quality of her caring and sensitivity and by her attention to the boundaries of a professional-child relationship. It was to become clear that Callum was of average intelligence, that he could still achieve well in school and that with some simple organisational measures he could find a way of surviving socially there, despite his reservations and anxieties.

Transitions

I then met Callum briefly at his father's house where once again he appeared briefly before running off to play in another room with two of his step-brothers. As had been the case with Mrs. Danang, his step-mother was blunt with me and clearly Callum could not have been oblivious to the level of hostility between these two women.

They shared not only reciprocal feelings for one another but a common language, full of the imagery of smackheads and perverts. Both Mrs. Danang and Callum's step-mother also shared an overt hostility to people such as myself. Neither were they enthusiastic about Callum seeing me on his own.

One part of the programme organised by Jenny for Callum was a twice weekly session at a Family Centre, which provided him with extra levels of care beyond school and opened up the possibility to him of other forms of adult support. An added advantage was that on those evenings he didn't have to go home so early. Eventually both Mrs. Callum and his step-mother agreed to let him meet me there, which was a place familiar to him.

Attendance at the Family Centre was not the only other form of support devised by Jenny; her last intervention was to organise Callum's transfer to secondary school. Mrs. Danang had not responded to the Local Authority's attempts to engage her in school selection and by default it had appeared that Callum would be on his way to the *sink comp*.

Jenny would not be transferring to secondary school with him, however, and she wanted to anticipate difficulties in his transfer. She worked tirelessly, obtaining his mother's agreement and signature and persuading the Local Authority of Callum's overwhelming need for the levels of support that would only be available to him at another local High School. Importantly, Jenny had predicted that the family name would not provoke quite the same negative reaction in this school.

By the time I met Callum again, nearly three months later, he had already been attending this new school for a month. I didn't ask him how it was for him but merely drew a simple scale along which 0 represented *awful*, moving to 5, *average*, OK and through to 10, which represented *brilliant*. With some enthusiasm Callum put his cross next to 10. I almost had no need to ask him this for he was as I had not seen him before – in a new uniform, clean, bright eyed and for the first time without his hunted look.

While he was never talkative at any stage, Callum did not seem discomfited at all and told me that seeing me was not a problem for him and also that he understood why we were meeting. At times he seemed to breathe out almost in sighs of relief while he voiced his thoughts and feelings about his family life.

Much of the detail of this meeting is not directly relevant to this chapter. However, it is important to know something of the gravity of the issues involved, in order to understand the significance of the eventual outcomes and professional responses.

Firstly, though, it is crucial to expose the power dynamic that occurs in any exchange between professional and child, whether the discursive setting be educational, social or familial (Billington, 2002). It is necessary to re-affirm that it is the adult's responsibility to understand the nature of the power relationship and to be able to reflect upon their own practice, as well as to subject it to peer scrutiny.

One way of working which allows the necessary sensitivity both to issues raised, as well as to the specific nature of the child's responses, is the act of listening or speaking to a child in conversation. It cannot just be any kind of talking to a child, however, since practitioner psychologists are expected to provide particular forms of evidence to the economic sponsors of their work, whether education, health, social services or in this case, the legal system.

In these conversations with children, the psychologist should have as a primary aim not to jeopardise the child's sense of safety but to provide a genuinely warm and supportive presence. Perhaps there is something here of Carl Rogers's 'unconditional positive regard' (1951). This, however, is not always possible, since the children often present an aspect of themselves that is difficult to like. At such times a more durable resource remains those Kleinian concepts of transference and counter-transference.

During such conversations children can often find it easier to discuss difficult issues when they are to some extent distracted from the intensity of the dyad itself. Some children enjoy drawing. Michael White's work with young people (e.g. White and Epston, 1990) in which narratives are developed that externalise the problem can also prove valuable but it is often possible to weave conversations with children in and out of the performance of what is in many respects an out-dated instrument, the *Bene-Anthony Family Relations Test* (1978).

The world has changed considerably since this test was conceptualised and the simplistic representations are often at odds with current ideas and values such as gender and culture. However, there are certain concepts which many children recognise and the value of the test is reflected by the seriousness with which a child invariably engages. One of its strengths is that, perhaps like those techniques based on Personal Construct Psychology (Kelly, 1955), the Bene-Anthony test allows children to deal with big issues in their life in a safe and emotionally containing manner (Bion, 1970).

The intention was to complete the assessment with Callum by providing him at all stages with a safe container for the strength of his feeling and thinking; anything else would be an abrogation of professional responsibility.

Listening to Callum

Callum first of all told me of the successful start he had made at his new school. The first mention of family to him, however, prompted his response 'which one'? During the next phase of our work he then expended much energy in trying to allocate his affections equally and fairly between his mother and father, re-affirming his wish to live with his father and mother on four nights and three nights respectively, each week. To the Court, this was at the core of the opinion required of me. I had to make a decision whether to ignore or embrace Callum's own wishes.

During our conversation he gradually opened up for me a vision of his home life with his mother which, when not portraying her being cross with him, was full of the nastier violence of other men towards her. At the mention of one particular man, Callum lowered his head as the tears fell down his cheeks. I merely asked him whether he thought this man was a good person and he quietly shook his head.

I also remember the story told to me by Callum's step-mother, who recounted an occasion when Callum had locked himself in the bathroom at their house. Evidently he emerged eventually to tell them of one particular incident at his mother's home in which he could remember his sister, Jade shouting hysterically 'no more... no more... Jimmy' to this man as he beat his mother yet again.

After our silence, Callum then spoke briefly but sensitively about his feelings of loss in respect of his sister whom he had not now seen for over a year.

Callum's views about his family were confused and his attachments diffuse. There seemed to be little holding him together emotionally other than his own heroic efforts. Despite all his other efforts, which were to remain loyal to his mother and to offer her whatever protection he could, and despite also those efforts to place his hope in his father, it was clear that Callum was now relying principally on himself. He was alone. He need tell me no more; the session could finish and I could write my report.

Clearly, however, there were positive things happening in his life, the contemplation of which would allow a more satisfactory transition for Callum at the end of the session. Indeed, I had already been told that, not only was he attending school regularly and punctually but he was also working hard and had joined several after-school clubs. He was still choosing not to go home. Thanks to Jenny, Callum now not only had the support of a new learning mentor but also the commitment of a Head of Year who had listened to her and who had put a plan into operation.

The Court wanted to know my opinion as to where Callum should live and of course he had told me that he wanted a split placement, four nights with his father and three with his mother. Problems here included the awkward and lengthy bus journeys this would entail should he live with his father during the week, with connections to be made at one of the city's bus stations, often at the end of a long school day. This was not a good scenario for a boy I considered extremely vulnerable in all sorts of ways.

At the professionals' meeting, the Local Authority took the position that Callum should live with his father and also that he should change schools. Clearly, there were problems with this, not least that Callum would continue to want to know that his mother and younger half-sister were safe by making regular visits. Also, despite his step-mother's claims, Callum's relationships with all the occupants of his father's household was at best lukewarm. His step-mother was later to tell me in no uncertain terms what she thought of this analysis.

It was my view, however, that the only aspect of Callum's life which was positive and to which he was now totally committed, was school. He was now attending school regularly, he was a member of several after-school clubs and he had confirmed these positive signs by his own description of school as brilliant. Given the uncertainties about a whole range of other issues in both homes, therefore, I decided to advise that, whatever decision was taken in respect of his residence, maintaining Callum's school placement should take precedence over all other issues as the first step in preventing his total exclusion from society.

This position invoked the scorn of one or two other professionals in-volved. To them, home was the most important issue. Well, of course, it was and is but the Local Authority as ever was hard-pressed for cash and was unable or unwilling to plough in the kind of resources which would be necessary to make it safe for Callum to live either at his mother's house or his father's. Financial constraints even pre-vented social services from fully accepting the significance of the issues raised by Callum himself in respect of both homes.

Nevertheless, I persevered and advised the Court that he had no secure foothold in either home and that it was only school that was preventing him from a life on the streets and moving beyond the margins completely.

A suggestion of a short-term foster placement was almost ridiculed for its naivety since the local authority was reluctant to consider this option, given both the cost implications and Government require-ments to meet targets on adoption. I was bluntly informed that the local authority no longer 'do fostering'.

The other professionals (Children's Guardian, social workers, solicitors, barristers and the Judge) seemed puzzled and then curious at the prospect of having to accept a child's education as a priority, rather than their residence with one parent or the other. The Court, however, did eventually accept my argument that Callum was attempting to anchor himself in school and to maintain a relationship with both his mother and his father. Social services were duly ordered to remain involved by facilitating and monitoring a dual placement with his mother and father which allowed him to continue at the same school.

Postscript

Callum has now completed nearly two years at his High School. The bright start he made was never going to be maintained to quite the same degree but he continues to attend and he has made very good progress in a range of subjects. Importantly, he continues to receive the whole-hearted commitment of several key staff who between them recently issued a glowing report. He even survived a period during which he encountered racist taunts and abuse.

Sadly, home issues continued to escalate as his step-mother indicated that she would only allow Callum's presence in her home under the terms of a full residency order in their favour. The local authority, however, at last paid heed to Callum's own reluctance to commit himself fully either to his mother or to his father. Unfortunately, it had been the intensity of aggression and threats of violence made to a number of their workers, rather than any propensity to listen to Callum, which prompted a change of position.

I suggest that it had been possible for this psychologist to listen to Callum's uncertainties about his parents but also listen in another kind of way to the commitment he was showing at school. I then used the power of my position to influence the Court's decision, which demanded that the local authority maintain a less straightforward solution for him: a dual placement, albeit with the balance of nights to be in favour of his mother (4:3) on account of practical issues of transport and safety.

However, it was the learning mentor's ability to listen to Callum, not merely to his spoken words but to the signals and context of his emotional disarray, that had been the crucial variable in this case.

Jenny did not offer counselling and neither did she press Callum to engage with her directly. It was her offer of a safe space into which he could enter quietly which ultimately enticed him to re-engage positively.

Many social services departments do not have sufficient resources to support children and their families. In such cases the extent to which schools contribute to social cohesion becomes clear to see. Indeed, it is more than this, for in the lives of many children whose families have either suffered breakdown or become dysfunctional, it is the school which can provide the last resistance to a permanent withdrawal or removal from society.

Schools clearly have many pressures of their own to withstand, targets to meet as well as other responsibilities. However, their more traditional, unheralded and indeed unquantifiable role as part of the fabric of community is becoming especially important, given the gradual erosion of other institutions such as local authorities and the church.

Due to the efforts of several hard-working education professionals, however, and perhaps even a government policy, Callum remains in school. This psychologist, the Children's Guardian, social workers and even the High Court Judge had played a part in resisting Callum's social exclusion. It would seem that external support workers can play a vital role in supporting school inclusion. Educational Psychologists, if given license to work in this way, are ideally placed to work across the professional domains of education and care and act as agents of inclusion.

On an individual basis, it is impossible to quantify the human value of Jenny's work. It is doubtful whether those employing her will ever quite have known both the pure simplicity and the sheer effectiveness of what a government policy will have first set in motion. Certainly spin doctors are not usually so fortunate as to witness such hope and possibility at the level of lived human experience. But then who would need spin if we were still prepared to value such work?

In a world which can often overwhelm us with its complexity, the scale of which can induce feelings of impotence, Jenny's work shows that we can all choose to resist exclusion and bring children back from the margins. Above all, her work demonstrates that we can each make a difference.

However, it had been Callum's own wish to place his school life as central and to maintain contact with both parents, even though this was not the most convenient of solutions for service providers. The value of the professional role was in listening to Callum and speaking with him in order that he might identify his own wishes as a mature reflection of his own self-interest.

It is up to the professional to advise how a young person's wishes can be addressed in safety.

4

How far from the margins? Reflections of an Educational Psychologist on a teaching experience with a child at the margins

Daniela Mercieca

This account of Adrian may be somewhat different from many of the chapters in this book. The aim of the book is to identify ways in which professionals can enable children to participate actively in decision making within their lives. This story is not that of a child, however, but of a former teacher. An educational psychologist recounts what happens with a boy with whom she had difficulty in class. There are three protagonists: the author, Adrian and the reader. Will you hear Adrian's voice?

Events take place in a classroom in a primary school in a town in Malta and although the country is different, the classroom is a space with which many readers will be familiar. Also, Adrian will not necessarily be an unfamiliar child to the reader. Empathy may arise from boys like Adrian who they have dealt with themselves, and the emotional conflicts which arise, both interpersonal and intrapersonal. Apart from the head on collision described here, from which both Adrian and myself emerge as losers to a certain extent, there is also a great deal of self doubt as I constantly questioned my intentions and actions. This piece of writing attempts to touch upon some of the complexities of the power struggle taking place, as the teacher tries emotionally and psychologically to contain the child, who refuses to allow himself to be contained (Bion, 1970). The container offered by the teacher is too unfamiliar and Adrian has learnt to mistrust the unknown. The teacher sometimes feels she can't handle the situation, and has the added burdens of dealing with feelings of panic and anger, as well as dealing with the child.

The style of writing chosen in this chapter is intended to reflect the content, as I have chosen to address the reader using the personal pronoun. The story is told as it happened, with the author still being very much present in that classroom while analysing the situation. The same feelings which were evoked while the story was taking place are allowed to re-surface, so that they and the events can be reflected on. I hope to present to the reader the complexity of the power struggle in this account, rather than the right or wrong of the issues. The interaction and difficulties between two individuals, each of whom sometimes struggles to survive in the enclosed space of a classroom, is what I hope to bring out. In today's society, one is easily alienated by many diversions and calls for attention and it is all too possible to lose oneself and forget how the well-being of the self is central to all one's activities. The *I* in this chapter reaches out to the I reading this chapter, and emphasis is placed on the necessity of a constant re-realisation and awareness that it is human beings, and not systems, with whom we work and live.

> It is the stories which I tell about my 'self' that identify with the 'other', while distinguishing my 'self' as 'another'; and it is precisely that dialectic which inserts 'me' (and which 'I' assert) within the experimental web of doing and suffering. (Nixon, 2001 p 225)

The above reflects a philosophy which is being explored in my doctoral work which is still ongoing. The reflexivity which underlies such thinking is that one needs to start with the self and address the needs of the self for an honest, non-alienating analysis of a situation to take place. Getting in touch with the *I* of the self is a prerequisite for getting in touch with the *I* of the persons with whom the self is working and living. It is a way of resisting alienation. Although the trappings of society and its systems provide a context for how situations develop, my aim is to keep in sharp focus that it is personalities who make up such entities and institutions. However, this book aims to develop a way of representing the voice of the child, and we therefore have to reflect also upon the nature of the processes of representation.

The story of Adrian and I

'I don't like school' was Adrian's contribution to the group discussion which I led on the first day of the Christmas term. It wasn't a challenge – that was to come later – it was just a statement then, a declaration of his state of being on that first day of school. I told myself that this was going to be my challenge of the year, to have Adrian's opinion of the schooling experience changed. I would manage to win him over as I had managed with last year's pupils.

But I still wince to this very day when I think of Adrian, of myself and Adrian in class. Now an educational psychologist, I draw on this experience to aid my understanding of teachers when they speak of children who are difficult in class, and also of the children themselves, as though through them I am given another chance of working with Adrian. We met while he was in Year 5, an intelligent boy who was very passionate about football and who had potential, both academic and otherwise.

However, although my intention and motives were of the best, we engaged in a mutual reinforcement of pushing each other away. Whilst being an active participant during classroom explanations, Adrian got bored with the monotonous exercises which were set and would often play the system and do the barest minimum. He had no pride in his work and would not do anything to oblige me, as other pupils would. Sometimes I would manage to challenge him and channel his interests towards the work at hand, but these moments were rare and not generalised to other areas. Adrian would be the first to ignore instructions of how something was to be done. While appreciating and encouraging the pupils to find their own methods of working, work of a lower standard was unacceptable and ultimately unfair to him.

As a teacher, I was constantly balancing being firm and being flexible with all my pupils and Adrian was no exception. However, he did not want to partake of this give and take relationship. He would not bargain and I wonder whether he even saw the possibility of bargaining. Adrian did not own the learning experience. For him, teachers were just there to make his life more boring, to make him do what he disliked doing. He did not seem to be able to see that my intention was to teach him and that his need was to learn. All he wanted to do was play football.

In a school where quite a large proportion of children could not read and write, skill in football was what was aspired to. The catchment area for the school was fiercely patriotic of anything belonging to the community. Football fever was very high at all times, with the successes and failures of the town's football team being the main topic of discussion during the season. The children were sometimes allowed to stay in the school yard and play football for a few extra minutes after break, especially those classes who had great difficulties in their schooling. However, the pupils in my class were sitting for national exams in the following year and the syllabus was very much based on the work done in Year 5. My pupils could not have extra minutes of play and conversation: they had the potential to succeed academically and it was my duty to help them fulfil that potential. The school, parents and most of the children also expected this of me. However, Adrian was one of those who did not think it was fair that we went indoors and worked while the others were outside playing. He was the only one who would not give in to my reasoning and persuasion. He would sulk for the rest of the day.

Sulking was something that Adrian did really well. He sat at his desk, trying very hard to maintain a scowl which must have taken great muscular effort to produce. He was never more unreachable than when he was scowling. I tried ignoring him, persuasion, ridicule and being stern. The situation would persist until a diversion came, such as break time, or even the end of the school day.

Feelings of helplessness vied with anger. How could this boy be reached? Why would he not give me a chance to redeem myself in his eyes? Why did he not want to redeem himself in mine? How was it that he did not seem to care at all for my good opinion? It was as though he had decided that things were not going to work out and was turning every situation into making sure that they would not. Every communication was becoming a point of contention. When this happened he would seem to turn into a hard rock as he seemed to expect me to try and break him. It wasn't him who was going to break: it was me.

In one incident on an outing, I was talking to him and explaining why he and his friends could not do something. It was an issue of safety and most children understand that such factors take priority over others. But I had only started to speak when Adrian took on the *rock* attitude. He put his head down and stood still, turning redder and redder with anger. After trying to speak with him, I realised he was even more incommunicable than usual because of his sun visor, which he was deliberately using to block me out. I asked him to look at me, and when he didn't, I asked him to remove his cap so I could see his face. When he did not, I removed it for him.

I was so frustrated that I could have shaken him, an impulse to which a professional is not supposed to admit. Taking his cap off was the closest I ever came to touching Adrian: it didn't matter that I didn't touch him. The context, the emotions felt and all the factors in that situation contributed to the meaning of my gesture. I was beside myself with anger at him for escalating the situation and at myself for playing along and doing exactly what he expected me to do. His negative idea of people in authority was reinforced: the aim of why I wanted to communicate with him was forgotten. It was replaced by my wanting to bend his will to mine.

But for me that would never be enough. I was not satisfied by him going through the motions for me, being forced to do so. I wanted to gain his trust, his understanding of my role and his, his realisation that what his teacher wanted was, ironically, not to bend his will to hers, but simply to learn to live together.

However, it was to get worse. One particularly exasperating afternoon, I did not feel I could take Adrian's scowls since I was having difficulty in containing my own anxieties. His brazen behaviour was infecting some other boys who also wanted to stay outside playing football rather than continue the lessons. Hoping to outsmart him, I told Adrian that he could go outside and play but that we were going to go on with the lesson. He cheered up instantly and tried to get some of the other boys to join him, but they would not. Although also rather difficult to handle, these others had their priorities in line with those of the school and they felt that in the long run it would be better if they stayed in class, since lessons were going ahead. Adrian grew redder and redder and finally decided to go outside and play by himself. He called my bluff: everything I was, everything I stood for, meant nothing for him. I failed.

My understanding of Adrian's reactions to me grew when his parents were summoned by the head teacher as his behaviour grew worse towards everybody in school. The behaviour I've described reflected the experience of everybody with the remotest semblance of authority. Adrian, his mother and father, myself and the head teacher sat round and spoke. His father was inclined to take umbrage with me as he mentioned an incident with a sun visor. Knowing that I also could be interpreted as being wrong in that situation, not because of what actually happened but because of the underlying dynamics of power and the frustration that I felt, I did not defend myself but explained how things apparently happened. I am very aware that I delicately manipulated my words to emphasise my need for visual contact when talking to Adrian on that day, rather than my anger. His father instantly took against Adrian and the emotional battering started, not of me but of Adrian.

My belief is that even if I went to the other extreme and just told his parents that I went plain mad and wanted Adrian to do what I said for once, just because I said it, his father would still have sympathised with me. He was the person who had probably most contributed to create that *rock* attitude in Adrian. He spoke to him very sharply, and, as Adrian started scowling, looking down and getting red, the father made him look at him, which Adrian eventually did, with his eyes full of tears of anger. His father's finger shaking in front of Adrian's face, he warned him against any such further behaviour and he poked a finger in Adrian's shoulder repeatedly and sharply to emphasise his words. Adrian had to sit there and take it all without reacting. It was his Dad who was the ultimate authority, and who did not break Adrian on this occasion only because he chose not to.

Compared to such strength, his teacher must have seemed very puny in Adrian's eyes. My professional restraint was seen as weakness and yet I was supposed to have the power to make him do things and to stop him from doing things he wanted to do. It may have been that Adrian perceived me as not capable of containing him (Bion, 1970) and thus not able to deal with his anger. And it was very possible that he was right in his intuition of his teacher's unreadiness for such a task. At that stage in my career development, I do not believe that I had the cunning, strength of mind, call it what you will, to provide Adrian with that safe container in which he could act out and yet be sure of a predictable response which he could handle. It seemed that his father's response, although probably rather an aggressive one, and one which would ultimately result in Adrian's submission to his father's ruling, was more welcome than my response, which I tried to base on understanding of Adrian's frustration. I was floundering and drowning as I tried to be kind on the one hand and resort to anger on the other.

As Adrian's tears overflowed down his silent face, I felt mine well up inside of me and fought hard with myself not to break down in front of everybody present. I felt such sympathy with the father's exasperation and anger, with the mother's sorrow and love, with Adrian's desperate need to be left alone.

What happened then? I think I gave up trying to save Adrian and concentrated on not making the situation worse. The only time when Adrian's and my attitudes approached one another was when his little brothers would run away from the infant part of the school to come and visit their big brother. This was a rare occurrence but I always welcomed the two little boys, while letting their teacher know that they were there. I would play with them a little and tease them. It helped create a bond between my children and myself: it was nice for us all to have something to laugh and feel good about together. On other occasions there would always be a few children who would not join in, but when Adrian's brothers came, everybody's attention was on them and we would spend a couple of minutes entertaining them until their teacher sent someone to take them back to class. Later, I would pass a remark to Adrian about his brothers. He would respond, and there would be a good feeling between us. I treasured these moments, rare though they were, and hoped that some impression was also left on him.

What had Adrian in the margins? What was keeping him there? He did not take on the work ethos of the classroom. Our priorities had no claim on him as he felt they were imposed on him and that he had played no part in forming them. His view was not sought at any time and the only thing he could do was react to them, because he did not want to comply with them. Since they were based on deferred gratification, they held no meaning for him. He wanted to experience the gratification of scoring goals in football and could not see the relevance of working hard in order to reap his rewards later.

Reflections on the within-without binary

This then is my experience. A respected mentor once recommended that I be not so overly sensitive or sympathetic but rather focus my energies on how such a situation came about and what could have been done in different circumstances. Experiences like the above haunt me, especially when I encounter an idea or a reading which encourages such reflection and thought. I can be sensible about it and say that this is just what every teacher goes through periodically and simply put it down to experience. However, the opportunity to write this chapter has encouraged me to mull over it and see the situation in *other* different lights.

The word *other* is purposefully italicised as it is what will prove helpful in my reflections about children at the margins. Thus far, the consideration has been placed on the binary of being within and without the margins. Adrian is beyond the margins of what is expected and accepted. He is chosen because he stood out among the rest of the children, most of whom were within the margins. Such children are often spoken of as ideal pupils or conforming pupils, with the respective connotations. Either way, pupils within the margins are seen in a more positive light than children without. Should we bring Adrian within the margins, have him conform more to his society's norms and values, to make him like the others? Or would it help to widen the margins for Adrian to be more comfortable in his position? How accommodating are the people around Adrian expected to be so that his wants and needs are met? Does Adrian have needs which he does not want to have met? Do we know better than him what is good for him?

These questions border on the philosophical and may never reach a conclusion, as I will later suggest. I believe it is important to consider the possibilities which such questions produce. We are often too eager to judge and label children and foist on them what might be our own problems of dealing with them. One possibility that is worth considering is whether Adrian is really like that, or whether he is just fulfilling a role in a classroom. When studying group dynamics, one notes who is the informal leader, the mediator, the joker, the person who protests? Such roles could also be present in the classroom and are adopted by some pupils. In taking over such roles, the pupils would also be taking on their shoulders the expectations that the roles carry as well as the accompanying perceptions and reactions to actions. This is why it may be very possible that Adrian and I kept reinforcing each other's positions: we may have both been too fixed in our respective roles in the classroom on opposite sides of the pole.

While other children seemed to have quite a clear sense of what was seen as right and wrong behaviour in a classroom and what would be advantageous for them in the long run, Adrian seemed totally oblivious. He did not even start to question what was right or wrong because he was totally absorbed in blindly fighting for what he wanted. There is a resemblance between Adrian and Kierkegaard's 'A' in *Enten-Eller* (Kierkegaard in MacIntyre, 1985), who chooses the aesthetic way of life, as opposed to the ethical way. Adrian was intent on losing himself 'in the immediacy of present experience' (Kierkegaard in MacIntyre, 1985, p 40). It took all his energy and he seemed to have no mental space left to consider that what I was saying to him might be motivated from a wish on my part for his good. The good that I wished for him was too far for him to see, too slow in coming. Adrian needed to see results now in order to connect them to his contribution towards them.

Children who are at the margins may not be able to take deferred gratification, or perhaps not at first. It might be a good idea to provide them with gratification which is more immediate, and yet which would be intrinsic so as to make the reward directly connected to the effort expended. Extrinsic rewards, such as stars, are objects which can be attained through various means. I think we should try to attract children at the margins towards the good feeling that can be attained through achievement, which feeling can only be attained through effort. Perhaps such good feeling would be a substitute for the pleasure which is at hand when one chooses the aesthetic route (Kierkegaard, *ibid*). Once hooked into that good feeling, they might feel some semblance of motivation in order to maintain it, and thus start considering life in terms of the rewards of the ethical. Here, Adrian's choice would be different; in following the ethical route, he would be leaving the aesthetic (at least with regards to schooling) and start considering his actions in terms of good and bad, in terms of deferred gratification. Thus Adrian might start to think about how his effort would eventually lead to good exam results and a better life style.

Then Adrian might gain a better understanding of the helpful role of the teacher in class, rather than only the disciplinary role. He did not seem to be socialised into listening to what others had to say and could not concede any point in others' perspective. That would have meant that he would lose. Perhaps if, in his father's speeches, there were more chances for Adrian to speak his mind and if he was listened to reasonably, Adrian could have learned to do likewise to others. However, this must have been a pattern of behaviour in both Adrian and his dad which they reinforced in each other. It was very much ingrained when I stepped into Adrian's life. One tactic that could have been adopted with Adrian was to take him by surprise one time and show him confidence in his views and concede to him points where he expected to be assaulted. Taking people by surprise in a positive way is very often quite effective to change perception. Their defences are less securely guarded for a few critical moments, in which time a new perception can be formed. If it is allowed to penetrate the thick skin formed after many years of failed communication, the possibilities thereafter are endless.

In this way children at the margins might be able to give and take, because giving would not mean weakness anymore and there would not be the threat of losing oneself because a little is conceded. Such an attitude as fairness would be better understood and not resented. Long erected defences might be lowered slightly and people who work with such children, such as teachers, might be given that half a chance to expose the children to an experience which is different, perhaps radically so, from what they are used to.

Reflections on the *Other*

The above considerations are all based on the binary around the margins. Children are meant to be within the margins, as that is how they succeed. Adrian was outside the margins and was giving me considerable grief as a consequence. This kind of binary is reminiscent of the peripheral and centre (Lefebvre in Soja, 1996) especially because of the spatial representation of margins with children within them or beyond them. This book focuses on children who are at the periphery, as opposed to those who are in the centre and who are managing to meet the social and educational demands made on them in their lives. We define children at the periphery by contrasting them to those at the centre and vice versa, almost in the method of contrast used in personal construct psychology to elicit more rigid definition on concepts. However, this dialectic reasoning risks the danger of being insular, and missing out on new, unanticipated possibilities (Soja, 1996).

> Two terms are never enough, [Lefebvre] would repeatedly write. *Il y a toujours l'Autre*. There is always the Other, a third term that disrupts, disorders, and begins to reconstitute the conventional binary opposition into an-Other that comprehends but is more than just the sum of two parts. (Soja, 1996)

Thus it would prove interesting and immensely useful to consider what the *Other* would offer. Which would be the third idea which would include both those within the margins and those who are marginalised, and yet be greater than the two put together? What would be the *Other*, which would 'as event, exceeds calculation, rules, programs, anticipations and so forth'? (Derrida, 1992)

This third idea, this *Other*, could be the child itself. This concept does fit and also tallies well with all the principles around which I base my present work and studies. No matter what the referral form tells me about a child, I try to make a point of seeing the child with as open a mind as possible, and to take from the child what she or he wishes to give me. No matter how much I try to understand Adrian at the margins, who put him there and what needed to be done to include him more, I will not get closer to understanding Adrian unless I see him as Adrian. The moment he told me that he hated school, I saw him as a boy who was a school hater and resolved on transforming him into a school lover, which may have clouded my vision as to who Adrian is in himself.

Supporting the teacher

How was I as a teacher to do this? Only just out of newly qualified teacher status, I was still relatively inexperienced, which may have been a factor. Being experienced does not mean that I would have moved away from categorising Adrian. It could very well mean that I might have been more judgmental and compartmentalising in my thinking. Perhaps it was my freshness as a teacher which allowed me to be reflective about my work.

However, my class would definitely have benefited from having a teaching assistant. I have experienced classrooms where another adult is constantly present and to whom the children can go, and the teacher's load was certainly much lighter. In Malta we have not yet started having teaching assistants in classrooms, except those who are directly assigned to a child with quite significant needs. They are called facilitators, according to the US model, and although it is part of their job description that they help with other children in class, in practice this very much depends on the disability of the child to whom they are primarily assigned. Moreover, we do not have Learning Support Teachers or Behaviour Support Teachers visiting our schools on a regular basis, as happens in the United Kingdom. A child who is presenting difficulties in class is really the teacher's problem, who can then ask the head teacher for help. Psychologists are very few and far between, which means that their focus is only on assessment and identification. The daily work with the child falls on the teacher's shoulders and the weight of this adds onto the already heavy load of a demanding syllabus and the needs of the other twenty odd pupils in class.

Slowly but surely, this situation where support for teachers is scarce is starting to change. But there are numerous participants and gate-keepers in the necessary policy formulating process (Fulcher, 1999). Thus, talks and discussions often end up at deadlock, leaving teachers struggling with all sorts of issues and difficulties, unsupported. Had the load been shared with other responsible adults, I might have been more able to distance myself from the issues with Adrian and to use some lateral ideas and thoughts to work with him differently, and allow him the space to be himself. I would perhaps have the chance to stop a little and reflect on the dynamics, perceptions and relationships both of the children and of myself working with these children. It is wonderful how one's perspective can change with such reflection, how uncooperative behaviour may seem reasonable in a different light, how children who are stubbornly at the margins are seen as children with valid justifiable reasons to be there. As it was, Adrian and his teacher were constantly re-defining each other as opposing poles, and this confirmed his idea that school had nothing to offer him.

The need to make schooling and education relevant to these children is vital and should be placed at the top of the list of priorities if the aim of the institution is to include such children. The distance between children and school has to be narrowed in a perceptible way for the children. This means that the participation of children and the expression of their voices has to be actively encouraged. One cannot have strong negative and positive feelings at the same time so that it is only when the anxiety associated with fear of failure is overcome that children can feel open enough to behave in ways to benefit their education. It is not enough to insert this aim as part of the policy of the school and to be complacent about its existence there. The onus has to be on the school to make this step, because this is what the school is there for. There needs to be a commitment on the part of the school to listen to the voices of marginalised children and groups and to make the experience of going to school meaningful to them.

It would therefore be advantageous and wise for schools to include children in the schools' policy making. The mere presence of them in the room when decisions are being taken on school policies is not enough. There needs to be a change in the attitude of school staff so that it becomes orientated towards children. Options have to be made available to children, the language used needs to be reviewed, as well as power dynamics which are implied and infiltrate every word and deed.

This may seem unrealistic and idealistic and disregarding of all the constraints which limit the actions of schools and the staff. And yet we may be approaching the point where we cannot afford not to be open to children's voices, to listen and take proper account of what they are saying. It is not right that the system which was created in order to help children now seems to work actively against them. In conclusion, the following analogy illustrates my view very clearly.

There was once a man who was sawing a tree trunk. He was working very hard at it and sweat was glistening on his skin as he hacked at the gnarled wood. His saw was blunt and it was giving him great difficulty as his effort had to be increased in order to overcome the obstacles the saw was providing. Another man who was passing by asked him why he did not sharpen his saw and thus increase its effectiveness. The first man replied, 'I cannot stop to sharpen the saw. I do not have the time.'

5

Listening, hearing and acting: Enabling children's participation through consultation

Stephanie James

Introduction

This chapter is concerned with the problematic nature of consultation with children and young people. It will argue that whilst the legislative framework to enable this to happen is now well established, building on the *UN Convention of the Rights of the Child* (1989), the evidence suggests that the outcomes are still more hoped-for rather than actual.

Particularly, the chapter will address the process of consultation with children and the competing dilemmas within the current education system relating to the twin aims of improving attainment and achievement while reducing social exclusion. Additionally, ways in which discourses reflect values within a society will be considered.

The chapter will also examine the social processes within education and suggest ways in which we might challenge theories and practices which marginalise or exclude children.

Finally, the chapter will provide suggestions for intervention and practice.

Current educational climate: inclusion or exclusion?

The educational climate within a society, primarily the political aspirations of successive governments, inevitably shapes policy and current mores. In a democratic society this is surely to be applauded. However, when policies appear to be shaped more by political expedience than reflecting the will of the population, it is time to ask hard questions. Just how much governments shape public perceptions and aspirations rather than reflect them is a matter for continued speculation. However, since children constitute a significant, disenfranchised population, it seems incumbent upon those who devise policies to consult with these consumers of the school system in order to take account of their views and wishes.

In other chapters Gamman and Pomerantz each argue, both explicitly and implicitly, that empowering children through involvement with curriculum goals enhances children's motivation. Others examine the overwhelming evidence that children are often mere pawns in government initiatives which, while purporting to be in children's best interests, are actually more concerned with presentation of data to indicate improving standards of schools and not improved chances for children.

While many children are indeed robust and manage to negotiate the competing demands placed upon them successfully, many others struggle to compete in what is essentially a market place, with all the attendant excesses of market forces.

Children are now routinely assessed and graded from their earliest days. By age 11 it is a rare child indeed who does not know very clearly whether they are a success or a failure in the eyes of peers and teachers. Consequent self-perceptions of competence have profound effects upon children's overall sense of worth (Ames, 1992; James, 2000) and significantly affect their engagement with the learning process and ultimately their life chances.

The thorny business of transfer to secondary school places children in the spotlight, with schools accepting and rejecting youngsters with no apparent concern for the emotional welfare of the casualties of the system. Of course, clichés are easy to find, for example, that this system prepares children for the reality of competition in the workplace, or that selecting children for their aptitudes and abilities is in their own interest. The reality is that when schools are competing for plaudits in the excellence stakes, children will always be used as tools and many will be emotional casualties.

The national and local newspapers routinely publish league tables of points gained by pupils in public exams. It does not take a mathematical genius to understand that if children are selected for aptitude and ability at the very beginning of the process, it is because their aptitude and ability will allow the institution to shine in the tables.

But what of the children who are not chosen? These children find themselves marginalised and are therefore most at risk of feeling and being excluded and disempowered. Further, whilst it will be argued that children who are already vulnerable in some way may be additionally discriminated against, there is also much evidence that by virtue of being children, all children are vulnerable to being used to score political points.

We can speculate upon the consequent effect upon youngsters' self-esteem of such absolute categorisation. The systematic and routine nature of such measurements, stat(e)istics ('the science of the state', Rose, 1989 in Billington, 2000), has become enshrined in the professional practice of many teachers and psychologists. Understanding that we, as professionals, are all capable of using statistical evidence to marginalise children is essential. Such reductionist models of ability have long since been discredited as potentially dangerous reflections of society's racial, class and sexual prejudices (Gould, 1981) and needs to be universally recognised.

Teachers and other professionals in the education system are becoming increasingly aware of the competing demands of the raising achievement and social inclusion agendas. It is easy to construct an argument that these apparently conflicting aims are not mutually exclusive. For example, it might be argued that setting individual goals for individual pupils will raise achievement in all pupils while celebrating the social inclusion of our most needy and special children.

This language is both patronising and disingenuous. Schools at the top of the league tables can of course afford to be generous and offer token places to needy and special children, so long as these children do not detrimentally affect the position of the school in the league tables. Other schools, whose brochures emphasise a strong social conscience, can also win plaudits by including the most needy children. Although at face value this seems laudable, one is struck once again by the underlying message which might subtly initiate a process of categorisation and marginalisation.

Children's voices can often be lost in adult rhetoric. But if we truly care about making a difference to the life chances of children we need to enable their full participation in the educational process. That means actively seeking their voices as full partners in the process. For without this partnership we will all be poorer, since learning is surely about everybody listening and acting.

Legislative framework and structures

Towards the end of the Twentieth Century there was growing international awareness that children had rights to express a view about any matter which affected them. This became enshrined in the oft-quoted UN Convention which stated that:

> Children, who are capable of forming views, have a right to receive and make known information, to express an opinion and to have that opinion taken into account in all matters affecting them. The views of the child should be given due weight according to the age, maturity and capability of the child. (Articles 12 and 13 *The United Nations Convention on the Rights of the Child*, 1989)

Quite clearly, how individual countries in a multiplicity of governmental and societal structures interpret these rights will largely be constrained by other structures in place within those societies, shaped by people's perspectives about how the world should and ought to be.

The British government's response to the growing awareness of the rights of children to have their views taken into account was reflected in the Children Act (1989). This required local authorities to ascertain the wishes of those children accommodated in public care and to encourage their participation in the assessment, planning and review process.

Within education, the Special Educational Needs Code of Practice (DfEE, 1994) made a tentative enabling statement, 'SEN provision will be most effective when those responsible take into account the ascertainable wishes of the child.'

It will be observed that this latter statement is not prescriptive but rather places the responsibility upon adults to interpret how one might take into account the ascertainable wishes of the child.

Other local and national government departments within education, health and Social Services have also responded to the growing movement to listen to, and consult with, children and young people (Quality Protects Programme, DoH, 1998; National Healthy Schools Standard, DfES, DoH, 2000; Health for Life, 2000). Each places significant importance on including young people in planning and decision making.

Most recently the revised Special Educational Needs Code of Practice (DfEE, 2002) takes this further, 'The views of the child should be sought and taken into account.' In the context of law the word 'should' means *must*. It is, therefore, incumbent upon us to ensure that both children and adults have the skills necessary for effective communication.

Reflective practitioners

It is evident that many teachers and others working with children and concerned for their experience of school are excited about the challenges posed in the business of listening to children. The value of reflective professional practices is clear and my work as a psychologist in supporting the process of realising such practice suggests that many professionals are anxious to explore the social processes which prevent and enable best practice.

I have been involved in several initiatives designed to ensure that adults working with children enable children's participation, in its widest sense, in matters concerning them. Particularly, I have led training sessions for teachers, foster carers, social workers and for multi-agency child protection professionals in which I have tried both to enable participants to understand the barriers to communication and to develop better ways of ensuring children's participation.

I intend to draw on two particular forums where the needs of children were discussed in relation to participation and consultation. One was a multi-agency Area Child Protection Committee (ACPC) working group, whose task was to produce guidelines for the inclusion of young people's views in the Child Protection (CP) process. This particular forum best illustrates the range of views from adults whose professional training routes are in many ways dissimilar.

The other forum was a series of Special Educational Needs Co-ordinator (SENCO) training sessions across two Local Education Authorities (LEAs) where SENCOs met to identify best practice to enable the requirements of the new legislation (DfEE, Code of Practice (COP) 2002) in relation to children's participation. The issues raised will be identified, and analysis of the processes at work will be offered. Finally, implications for practice are drawn.

I hope that as readers following this story you are able to apply the issues raised to your own professional context. Enabling children to participate in matters concerning them will have an impact upon their ability as adults to develop these skills further and so shape future generations' ability to participate successfully in society.

Although the people who are being written about are the adults whose role is to ensure that children's voices are heard, I shall also be examining the voices of some of the children as they reflect upon their experiences.

Discourses and Power

If one of the primary goals of child development is to reach a state of autonomy and self-actualisation (Maslow, 1954) then it is evident that the ability to participate in matters concerning oneself is of crucial importance to this goal. How can adults ensure that they take full account of the child's needs to participate? How, too, can adults ensure that they have the skills and abilities to listen actively to the child?

The adult participants in this chapter were largely a self-selecting group, each recognising the need to develop and implement the most effective practice for enabling children's participation. What also emerged was a willingness to recognise quite clearly that there are many cognitive, affective and pragmatic processes at work, which contribute towards enabling or preventing children's voices being heard.

Central to effective communication is a recognition that words do not always reflect the meaning given to them. At its most simplistic, we have all been caught off guard at some time and said 'yes' when we meant 'no.' How more problematic does the position become when youngsters are asked to give reasoned answers to complex questions. Consider children who are asked to listen to a lengthy explanation from a powerful adult, a teacher or someone else in authority. That adult explains how, why and when something will happen, followed by the question, 'is that OK?' The likely reply, 'Yes,' reluctant or otherwise, is almost inevitable. If children answer in any other way, they risk exposing themselves to a minefield of negotiation for which they are neither skilled nor practised combatants. This is neither consultation nor participation. Worse, it risks actually causing more harm than good. Asking for someone's view when the answer is apparently already prescribed risks the charge of abuse of power.

There is a further argument which suggests that what people say is not only shaped by the language they use. *Foucauldian Discourse Analysis* (FDA) (Willig, 2001), is a way of analysing dialogue which is not concerned only with the words which are spoken, nor with how the words are strung together. Nor is it so much concerned with the other aspects of language that infer meaning, for example, tone of voice or pauses and unfinished sentences. It goes much further and asks fundamental questions about how people think and feel and how this relates to what they do. Foucault (1982) exposes for us links between discourses and social processes, in particular relating to issues of power and legitimising actions. Thus, the ways in which adults construct children's voices can in themselves affect how these voices are heard and acted upon.

In any adult dialogue, opportunities for misunderstanding are multiple. The divorce and separation rates in our country support this claim and are particularly good examples since presumably these adults enter into marriage or partnership with commitment and adequate communication skills. Why, then, should we be particularly surprised that communication between adult and child is fraught with opportunities for misunderstanding? Whilst not all communications should be subjected to in depth psychological analysis, an awareness of the processes at work is essential.

Central to this is an understanding that people's construction of reality (Harre, 1986) emanates from a synthesis of their experience and personal constructs. Such experience includes people's individual life histories of what *should* and *ought* to be the case, together with influences exerted by, for example, their own professional training. Again, whether people understand the world to be socially constructed; whether the reality in each person's perception is constrained only by the meaning they or society as a whole place upon it, is important to explore. Others may see the world from a positivist standpoint, being as it is because of some preordained or prescribed criteria.

Another aspect which influences the individual is what he or she understands as the resolution of conflict between one person's or organisation's rights and another's. Children, too, are not immune from constructing their own version of reality and their own views about what should and ought to be.

Additionally, there are the constraints of legislation, not least those which come from the UN Convention itself. Further layers of complexity, for example within the child protection arena, might also result in the voices of children going unheard. Within that forum, adults, usually the child's parents or carers, have the right to be heard and to be involved in decisions taken about their children. Abusive adults frequently continue to deny their involvement in a child's abuse, even when a court has made a finding of fact about their culpability. How do the rights of these adults conflict with those of children to know what is being said about them, to be involved in the process of solution management and especially to be protected from further emotional abuse which such denial might lead to?

If one adds to this the pragmatic, practical considerations of what is possible within certain time frames and budget allocations then the potential difficulties become evident.

The conflicting needs of any organisation must be weighed carefully against the needs of individuals. But who is to decide, on a case by case basis, whose needs are paramount? And what of the decision makers' own spheres of influence?

It may be at such points of conflict, if not before, that individuals might turn to research for guidance. Then there is the issue of managing conflicting research evidence and how to legislate for the weight each individual gives to any one piece of research over another. The opportunity to engage reflexively in ordinary decision making might result in more enabling practice.

What might follow are the natural threats and opportunities which arise in any organisation, including the threat of offence to one party or another and the consequent fall-out from decisions that are taken. Imagine a situation when a decision taken in favour of the child may be seen by some as a decision against an adult or organisation. What is the natural default position? Evidence suggests that at points of conflicting evidence, children's voices are largely unheard and that, worse;

> Child witnesses are a spanner in the works because, in our culture, it is easy to maintain a default assumption that adults are competent while it is very difficult to maintain a default assumption that children are competent (Hutchby and Moran-Ellis, 1998). One has to test a child's competence... (Lee, 2003, p 48)

Overcoming professional differences, biases and barriers

Within both the SENCO training sessions and the CP working group there was evidence of different professional training routes having an impact upon the perceptions of individual participants. Some participants saw children as partners, others as clients. Still others saw children as needing protection from difficult decisions.

Individual styles of persuasion expressed within the groups had different effects. Statements beginning 'research has shown' seemed to have an impact upon the views about how old a child should be before his or her word is given due weight. That conflicting evidence was not also weighed demonstrates the dangerousness of selective use of evidence. In an age when research is often funded by interest groups, it should not be surprising that selective findings are used to support practice. There may be many reasons for this: A belief in a principle can be shored up by use of selective, ill conceived or rogue research. Secondly, selective evidence can be used to back a current stance since any other view might challenge authority or expertise. In either of these situations an opportunity for real growth and development is obscured.

Elsewhere in this book Lown has illustrated ways in which systems theory has implications for multi-agency working. Often, role confusion, territorial protection and inconsistencies between duties and policies of different agencies prevent adults from co-operating. All too often children may once more be victims of these communication barriers between adults.

Current government initiatives encouraging multi-agency working (Every Child Matters, DfES, 2003) make it crucial that adults from different agencies work effectively together. Therefore, the ability of professionals to seek together for a range of evidence and to review this appropriately is vital. Failure to do so makes children vulnerable. Worse, it is a further betrayal, since what is then is carried out is in the name of 'enabling participation'.

Selective use of evidence is a clear example of the possibility of professional dangerousness. Other patterns of this were evident initially through exaggeration of hierarchical knowledge and expertise and closed professional systems. However, it became possible to offer some moderation by agreeing to elicit a consensus view about what were essential elements to children's participation.

Ensuring the focus here was upon the needs of the child rather than on the needs of professionals, organisations or carers was paramount. The adults were eventually able to construct a list of children's needs and rights, leaving aside some of their own professional biases. This was heartening and is an example of what is possible when children's needs are seen by all as of greater importance than professional boundaries.

Essential considerations for effective consultation

What follows is a synthesis of what emerged as the essential elements necessary to inform proper consultation with and participation of children in matters affecting them.

If we are to expect children to make informed decisions about what happens to them, it is essential that they are given age appropriate information. This means using familiar language which the child can understand. Gaining feedback from the child and giving them clear messages that they are being listened to are also important.

Often we expect children to voice their opinions orally with the same ease as adults do. Giving thought to allowing and enabling an opportunity to express feelings or views in whatever medium is appropriate, for example, drawings or in play, might result in effective communication for children who have difficulty articulating their thoughts and feelings. Adults must be aware of the pitfalls of poor interpretation of all forms of communication. Asking a child a question and then failing to explore the answer adequately is worse than not asking at all.

All of this is time consuming but allowing sufficient quality time to elicit these views is essential. However, it is not essential for an adult to help a child to articulate their thoughts. This might be more appropriately done by a peer whom the child trusts, and who is likely to have a very good level of communication with them. In this way thoughts and feelings can be rehearsed, polished and distilled. No matter how much a child says and how carefully an adult listens, adults in authority will always retain most power. Nevertheless, allowing children to control the content and pace of dialogue can help redress the balance.

One of the SENCO training tasks was to talk to children about their experiences of consultation. Feedback suggested that there was overwhelming evidence that children felt that an enabling school ethos was vital, where this was categorised as one of mutual respect and openness. One child gave an example of how this had been demonstrated to him on his first day at secondary school when the teacher had said that he must speak out if anything was worrying or concerning him. She had said, 'If you're happy we're happy'. For him, this one exchange lowered anxiety and gave him the confidence throughout his school career to express his views.

Other children thought that the most important factor was that school staff were willing to be flexible. These children felt that, although they wanted to be treated the same as others and 'not stand out in the crowd', slight variations in what was required of them could have enormous benefits. This can be unsettling for teachers since, by definition, flexibility results in some loss of control. However, this flexibility can lead to enormous benefits on all sides.

In many situations where communication is at its most difficult, the root of the problem may lie in poor or inadequate understanding of the terminology. Many children said that they were better at making their views known and understood when they understood the jargon used in reviews or target setting. It is easy to assume that because phrases are in common parlance in a particular group everyone understands them. Again, careful checking and feedback can prevent potential misunderstanding.

One boy, who was profoundly deaf, found it difficult to give his views when he hadn't ever before been asked to contribute to reviews. Parents and teachers wanted him to go to a boarding school from the age of fourteen, whereas he wanted to remain with his friends at his current school. The boy reported his absolute sense of helplessness as the adults around him discussed his needs within the framework of a formal annual review of his Statement of Special Educational Needs. His lack of understanding of the terminology, the adults' clear familiarity with the format of the review, and sheer weight of numbers all conspired to suppress his voice. When asked why he didn't speak up he said 'What was the point? I hadn't had any practice in saying what I wanted and knew that I wouldn't be able to say it right so I just agreed with them.' Whatever argument of best interest might be constructed to explain the adults' actions, the fact remains that, for this youngster, helplessness was the overwhelming outcome.

When other children were asked, they said that they liked to attend meetings about them so that 'there are no surprises' and that they 'can hear what people are saying' about them. They preferred this even when they disagreed with what was being said about them. However, they also said that they liked to negotiate and that even when a decision was reached which they did not wholly agree with, the very fact that they had been consulted was important to them. What seems to be crucial is finding ways to demonstrate that adults truly value children's opinions.

Another impediment to communication in all forums is anxiety, such that the ability to give and receive accurate messages is acutely affected. We need to understand what provokes anxiety in children. It was heartbreaking to hear a boy say that he hated attending SEN reviews because his mother didn't know about his disability. It transpired that his mother had always tried to hide her concern from him and so hadn't ever alluded to his problem. He had cerebral palsy. By the same token, the boy was so concerned to protect his mother from what he saw as his problem that he, too, never mentioned it. In fact, he thought his mother didn't know about it! Clearly, this illustrates one of the pitfalls of poor communication and the need to appreciate the differing perceptions of children and their parents to the problem. Both are valid and equal points of view. The skill is in ensuring that the child's viewpoint is given equal status.

Issues for practice

This chapter has illustrated some of the factors which enable or prevent effective participation of children in matters affecting them. It has looked particularly at the impact upon those children within the child protection and special needs processes. However, the principles are the same for all children.

The common thread is that of empowering children and understanding that we, as adults, exert enormous power merely by being adults.

There is no doubt that many adults whose task is to listen to children are striving to be more effective in enabling children to participate in all matters affecting them. The will is there and many of the skills are in place. Certainly, that was the experience of many of the children who were asked. However, there is no evidence that this is routinely the case. Where there are competing requirements of curriculum, attainment and inclusion goals the temptation is to consult less and demand more. The reflexive approach adopted by the adults charged with consulting children is crucial. Success appears to be dependent upon adults continuing to ask themselves a series of questions, a checklist for successful communication.

- Do I have the ability to hear the voice of the child? How do I know?

- Are the structures within my organisation flexible enough to allow the child's wishes and views to be taken into account? If not, how might I manage or change this?

- 'I asked and the child said nothing.' Do the children in my care have the power to create opportunities to make their voices heard? How can I improve my practice?

- Do I appreciate the complexity of the learning context? What impact do perceptions (e.g., the roles of psychologist, school, parents, teachers' children) have upon the voice of the child?

- Are adults and children in agreement about what the problem is? What role does the construction of the problem have upon the ability of adults to hear children? How can I ensure that each is given due weight?

- Are any of the targets abusive or disempowering? For example, children who have difficulty in relating positively to peers might appear aggressive. An appropriate target might be seen by some as to become less aggressive. How might this further alienate the child from those with whom he or she is having most difficulty relating? And why does that child have such difficulty?

- Do words truly reflect thoughts and feelings? How can I be sure that what the child is saying accurately reflects their views?

Asking these kinds of questions ensures that we as adults remain aware of the barriers to communication. It is tempting to believe that because we talk with children on a daily basis we are good at it. This practice-makes-perfect assumption must be constantly challenged if we are to remain vigilant to the possibility that our power is standing in the way of effective communication. In a culture where children are often used as political pawns, it is essential that we become more adept at finding, listening to and acting upon the voices of children. Asking these questions will ensure that we remain alive to the possibility that there is action which we can take to improve our practice and so improve the children's chances.

6

Separating children for inclusion?
The effectiveness of Nurture Groups
(NGs) in early behaviour support:
Some problems in seeking pupil views

Brian Willis

The paradox of intervening with early behaviour difficulties by separating pupils from their peers so that they can make gains with social and emotional skills is at the heart of the inclusion debate. Whether students who display challenging behaviour should be educated in a mainstream or segregated placement is high on the current educational policy agenda. Often these are vulnerable children, who function at the margins within school settings and who run the risk of being labelled and rejected at an early age. I argue that decisions about inclusion should usually be made on a values basis and research cannot offer ready solutions. DfEE policy, as described in publications such as *Social Inclusion: Pupil Support* (DfEE, 1999) and *Promoting Children's Mental Health within Early Years and School Settings* (DfEE, 2001) state that appropriate planning and intervention, together with early involvement, are crucial. The dilemma between raising achievement and promoting inclusion is ever present and NGs have been seen as an important approach in addressing such issues.

Within my own Local Education Authority (LEA), the approach for dealing with more extreme adjustment difficulties has traditionally been to look towards segregated placement in a Pupil Referral Unit (PRU), often for pupils as young as five or six years of age. More recently, however, the segregated placement of pupils in Key Stage 1 has been discontinued and NGs within individual schools are seen as an alternative. To what extent, however, do we actually listen to pupils to encourage them to participate and give views about this provision? This chapter seeks to focus on the effectiveness of NGs and to listen to the voices of children who are selected for placement in such groups.

There seems to be a prevailing view that young people's behaviour is getting worse and that NGs are a useful way of addressing the problem. However, it is important that we ask about the theoretical basis for such approaches, such as the assumptions they make about parents and how they interact with their children. In addition to asking whether such interventions are effective, we need to consider whether they are appropriate for all children with additional social and adjustment needs. Are these approaches segregationist and are we simply labelling pupils and parents at an early stage and paving the way for further 'separating, losing and excluding children'? (Billington, 2000)

Billington (*ibid*), when discussing the ways in which children can be pathologised, provides an historical account of the ways in which professionals continue to devise new technologies which 'map shifting constructions of abnormality and thus contribute to the industrialisation of human differences'. Are NGs simply an example of a new technology, which creates difference? Rose (1989) has seen children as the most 'intensively governed sector of human existence' and the question arises as to whether we are now targeting children earlier for new forms of governmentality and control? In Burden's chapter on respecting the voice of the child in translating values into rights in Lindsay and Thompson (1997), he notes that by 'focusing on the needs of one or another minority group or even on the shifting needs of the majority may well lead, paradoxically, to a denial of their rights'. By emphasising early intervention and, therefore, identification of need, do we in fact run the risk of creating negative expectations for pupils and parents, particularly when some form of segregation from the pupil's mainstream class is involved? For these reasons we need to ensure that any possible segregatory intervention, such as a NG, is demonstrably effective and adequately supported to ensure sustainability.

The paradox of identifying a child's needs and simultaneously allocating stigma raises many issues if we are to meet the needs of all children. How can all children follow a standard curriculum, where the emphasis is on achievement in literacy, numeracy and science? There needs to be an increased recognition of the different and varying levels of social and emotional maturity of pupils and their corresponding needs. Pupils can then be taught in ways which reflect and match these needs. Such considerations go beyond the number of hours of support a child receives, but include a willingness to set up accepting and diverse support systems. Billington has described how a Learning Mentor set up support systems for Callum, which recognised the vast gulf between his world and that of the school, and provided him with space and choice to make some tentative steps towards learning.

Schools are often reluctant to look into the social and emotional world of the child and need structures which give them the rationale, time and encouragement to look beyond mechanistic core National Curriculum subjects. Whilst systems do exist for looking more closely at social and emotional skills, what is lacking is a perception that such perusals are necessary, even if they do not fit in with the measures on which schools and pupils are currently assessed.

The Need for and Prevalence of NGs

Similarly, NGs seem contrary to the inclusion agenda in that pupils are removed from their own classrooms. This may have led to a decline in their popularity during the 1990s. More recently a national NG network is assisting with accredited training and support. Courses are run in London and Cambridge while Leicester University is a national research centre. The link between social problems and economic deprivation has led to the establishment of NGs in Inner London boroughs like Enfield and also in Newcastle. Changes in educational policy have been accompanied by large increases in exclusions from schools in recent years and both pupil background and school factors have contributed to the rebirth of NGs.

According to recent research from Paul Cooper (2002) there has been a rapid expansion and between a half and two thirds of education authorities have NGs. Provision level now varies considerably between authorities so that around 50 LEAs have one group, whilst a single LEA has 50 such groups. Some schools recognise the importance of NGs and are driven by the commitment of practitioners to their principles and values. Such practices appear to be in line with the suggestion made by Billington (*op cit*), that 'professional energies might be channelled rather towards practices which seek to minimise some of the more punitive effects of social exclusion.'

Personal involvement

My own involvement in the area of NGs began in 1997, when together with the Headteacher and the school Educational Psychologist (EP) a Mental Health Foundation (MHF) multi-agency project was set up to support the development of whole school approaches to early behaviour difficulties in a Doncaster school. Health Service staff were also involved and students from two local EP training courses helped with project evaluation, which has been well publicised nationally. Significantly, school staff felt that the NG was the most effective of the approaches used.

Initially a therapeutic and less structured approach was envisaged, though school staff adopted the method used in Enfield, including the Boxall profile evaluation instrument. These profiles have been a cornerstone of the Nurture Group approach and are described by Bennathan and Boxall (1996). In the Doncaster study, two thirds of the pupils involved were seen to have benefited significantly on these scales from the intervention and teacher views were positive. Pupil and parent views were not investigated and differential longer term pupil responses were not considered. The group ran for only one half day each week and so tried to approximate the Enfield or real NG model. It was acknowledged that further funding and support would be required to make such an intervention sustainable and there was a need to involve the parents of the pupils in the group.

Considerable publicity regarding the project followed within the LEA, and the wider dissemination of the NG and parent support group approaches has been an outcome. Despite funding availability, the reality is that in October 2003 only two schools within a large Metropolitan Borough run Enfield model NGs and this remains at the level of one weekly half day. There are issues around competing demands, staff funding, planning and providing a base for the group. Major support initiatives would be necessary to tilt the achievement and inclusion balance towards wider use of such an intervention. Doncaster established a Senior EP post to lead the development of early behaviour support, utilising the nurture and parent group support methods to promote inclusion and move away from the previous segregated PRU provision.

The Nature, Ethos and Structure of NGs

NGs are seen to provide early experiences which some children may have missed and are based on the belief in a need to establish attachment with an adult figure. Bennathan and Boxall state:

> ...in the NG the teacher and helper attempt to relive with the child the missed nurturing experiences of the early years. They take as their model the mother and her young child and the method is correspondingly intuitive: the teacher and helper 'feel into' the early years and interact with the child as a mother would within a relationship of continuing care and support, in an environment that is carefully managed and protective. (Bennathan and Boxall, 1996, p 20)

Boxall (2002) sees the aim as providing the restorative experience of early nurture in the child's neighbourhood school and as enabling pupils to see themselves as distinct individuals in relation to other people. In NGs workers interact at a developmentally appropriate level with children and demonstrate appropriate social behaviour, such as waiting or taking turns.

Paul Cooper has used the concept of 'real NG', as not all NGs are 'real NGs'. 'Real NGs' have a developmental emphasis, are a part of integrated provision and use particular diagnostic and evaluative tools. NGs are usually at Key Stage 1, though they are sometimes used at Key Stage 2, with Key Stage 3 groups being rare. Detailed assessment methods determine starting points and targets, enabling work at the child's level. Real NGs incorporate the features of the Boxall NG with ten to twelve pupils, a teacher and a trained support assistant and they function for nine out of ten half days each week. Play is encouraged, a learning curriculum is evident, social learning activities are available and there is an opportunity to eat breakfast together. The quality of interaction between the child and other children and the adult and child is important, with less emphasis being placed on control. The two workers model appropriate social skills.

Groups like the Doncaster one may not be classic in form but are classic in function, adopting the above values, but do not have nine half days. Some off-site groups create the classic group approach and maintain mainstream links. There are also groups which are not classic in form or function, but which do provide a nurturing environment. The provision might be infrequent and may run over lunchtime for one or two hours weekly.

Other groups are not classic in form or function and do not do a nurturing job. These are 'sin-bin' groups, segregated from the mainstream, which run the risk of damaging pupils by separating, excluding and stigmatising them. The stringent requirements of 'real NGs' expose the punitive nature of other such groups.

Area NGs

Exclusionary pressures in schools often force LEAs to make segregated provision which takes pupils out of their local school. Two such NGs were set up in a poor area of Newcastle in the mid 1980s and were described by Keith Hibbert and others in Bennathan and Boxall (1996). The process of segregation was contrary to the fundamental need for schools to own the group and for the ethos of the school to be influenced by the group. Willis (1994) described the crucial importance of school ownership of behaviour policies and approaches.

LEA staff ran the Newcastle units and various problems emerged with staff appointments, admissions criteria and procedures. Maintaining the initiative was not possible, despite early staff commitment to the Enfield model. School funding changes, increases in class sizes and admission of pupils with more extensive needs led to difficulties. The group ethos and co-operative working relationships between unit and school staff were not maintained.

Can the true ethos of a NG be maintained where a catchment area wider than the host school is used? Ideally, a school needs to retain responsibility for its pupils, by maintaining the involvement of the class teacher and promoting a positive interaction between all school staff which is consistent with its desired ethos. The NG might then be able to support such a positive ethos.

Examples of NG use

In my research I found various forms of NGs in the same locality. Two classic Boxall groups had been set up in one city with support from outside agencies. In a nearby borough, two school groups were supported through Standards Fund money and were run by school staff. In another borough, however, a group took the majority of its referrals from social services, with the drawback that the NG was less of a school owned resource.

In another city a shared teacher post was used to support a NG for a group of schools, in which pupils could stay for up to five terms. Here, a multi-agency LEA steering group is in place, though liaison and transfer of pupils between schools is often difficult because teacher perceptions of students vary. There are also concerns about longer term funding of provision as the project is a Standards Fund LEA pilot.

In one county the Behaviour Support Service runs some NGs and support is put into a school for a term, with the groups running for four afternoons and having a balance of pupils. One group runs on a full-time basis, and a Key Stage 2 group exists for some Y3 and Y4 pupils. Goodman questionnaires and Boxall profiles are used, with targets being set and monitored and parent perception schedules used. Full class circle time sessions maintain peer group contact and address salient social curriculum issues.

An exploration of what young children think about being in a NG

I attempted to obtain the views of pupils in the Doncaster school which carried out the above MHF project. It has continued to provide a NG for one half day each week, though because of funding difficulties it has been managed by two nursery nurses. The group catered for reception pupils generally and about ten pupils were involved, with some reserves in case of absence. In order to listen to the voices of the children involved, attempts were made to obtain their views about the group, their mainstream class and their perception of why they were selected for it. Other questions were asked about the children's perceptions of separation and difference, and about how they saw the benefits or otherwise of such provision.

An educational psychology student asked questions designed to elicit information about their likes and dislikes in the group. In addition, they were asked about how it was helping, why they were in the group and how they would feel if it stopped. Questions also tapped pupils' views about the difference between and preference for the NG in relation to the mainstream class. These questions were asked in a circle time setting through the staff, with follow up from myself. Use was made of video and audio tape recording, with the student using the video recorder for the group discussion. After the whole group discussion children were asked, individually, what they thought about the relationship between the two workers during a pizza making activity.

Naturally, I was aware of the probable difficulties with understanding involved in ascertaining the views of such young children so questions were made simple and were repeated. The language comprehension and expression skills of reception class pupils can be limited and the level would vary between pupils. Furthermore, in a group setting, social and emotional skills would be immature, so that turn taking, listening, expressing feelings and waiting would be difficult. The level of intellectual development made some concepts involving comparison or preference difficult. Often pupils in such groups are less advanced than the average pupil of their age and there is a need to consider the age at which it is developmentally realistic to obtain pupil views at all.

NG staff and EP colleagues were consulted about the nature of the questions and method of delivery for the four or five year olds. Draft questions were discussed with the two staff some time before the session and their views on the best way of eliciting information were sought. The group contained a balance of boys and girls with a range of abilities and despite the careful preparation and simple language used, several pupils still had great problems understanding the questions. One pupil, for example, was always very keen to raise his hand, but was not able to answer. One girl was quite able in terms of language comprehension and acted as a leader for the group. We did, however, try to guard against others copying her views, by getting them to take turns to answer questions.

In terms of the language complexity involved in the questions, the pupils had difficulty with negatives; for example, 'What don't you like about being in the Fun Club?' This was the name chosen for the group by the pupils. Also, abstract ideas, thoughts and concepts such as *different* and *preferred* were not easy for some pupils, even though the questions were asked in the format 'What do you do here that you don't do in the main classroom with (teacher's name)?' and 'Do you like to be in your main class more, with (teacher's name)?'

Despite these difficulties, it was clear that the children generally liked both the NG and their own class. They believed that the NG helped them to play and to make more friends. All the pupils had difficulty in expressing why they had been chosen for the group but this is not surprising, given their age and the complexity of the concepts of social and language skill development. Some positive feedback was obtained: when asked how they would feel if the group stopped, the children were generally able to say that they would be 'sad'. One child, however, did say 'happy' and it was difficult to know whether this reflected an honest feeling or whether it was because he didn't fully understand the question. Interestingly, the adults assumed that his reply was due to a lack of comprehension, even though his command of language was quite advanced. When asked what they would miss about the group if it stopped, the children mentioned 'cooking and play' and several said that they would not be happy about this.

We did try to draw out the views of the children on the relationship between the two adults in the NG. Other than saying they felt they liked each other, because they talked to each other it was difficult to draw out significant issues, such as how the children felt towards them or how they demonstrated appropriate behaviour. Nevertheless, it was clear that they did like both the NG and their class and that the opportunity for play was appreciated.

The cautionary tale of Darren

One pupil, Darren, was assigned to the group session as the staff were collecting pupils from their classes. He was a year older than the other reception year children and was also much bigger and generally seen as boisterous. His teacher said that he had been having a difficult week, because his father had left home, but thought that the session would benefit him and would also give the rest of the class a break from his demanding behaviour.

During the initial stages of the session I did not really notice Darren, because my attention was directed to the practical matters of recording, discussing questions and joining in with the circle time activities. However, it soon became evident that Darren was not happy about being in the group. He sat with his head down, participating only reluctantly when asked questions directly and banging on the floor with his feet. He was a much bigger and older boy, who seemed to sit defiantly in his rugby shirt. He stood out in the group as being different from the other pupils and obviously did not want to be there. Eventually, despite many attempts to engage him, he was taken back to his class. Such a scenario illustrates the way in which such groups can be misused and run the risk of exacerbating difficulties for the pupils. What Darren communicated quite clearly was his resistance to being in the group.

Research into the effectiveness of NGs

Because of these difficulties involved in obtaining the views of young children, it is also necessary for us to listen to the voices of the adults involved and to consider assessment schedules, which can provide information on skills, targets and progress. The Boxall profile consists of a number of strands and include developmental and diagnostic tests, which include areas of difficulty.

More recent work by Paul Cooper (2002) looks at the effectiveness of NGs in promoting social, emotional and educational functioning. Mainly classic groups were investigated, being taken from 23 NGs in eleven LEAs and both new and old groups were used. Samples of matched pupils in mainstream NG schools, with and without emotional and behaviour difficulties (EBD) were used. Also, matched pupils from schools with no NG, with and without EBD were considered. The design involved testing on entry to the group and after two or three and four terms. All children were assessed on the Goodman Strengths and Difficulties Questionnaire, which was concerned with behaviour in mainstream. NG children were also assessed on the Boxall Profile and interviews with staff, pupils and parents were carried out.

Effects on behaviour and pupil differences

In Cooper's research, children in NGs improved on behaviour ratings. This was most marked after two terms, with more established groups doing better. On the other hand, the behaviour of pupils with EBD in schools without NGs deteriorated over two terms and EBD pupils in NG schools did better than all non-NG pupils. Boxall profile data shows more pupil engagement and purposeful attention and pupils engaging with peers and appearing to become better learners.

The five Goodman (1997) subscales include pro-social, hyperactivity, emotional, conduct and peer problems. Strikingly, all pupils categorised in these ways do well in NGs. However, the social/ emotional and hyperactive groups do not generalise their improvement to mainstream classes. Pupils with social and emotional difficulties, where improvements are not generalised often complained of ailments, had many worries, were unhappy, nervous or clingy and were easily scared. One conclusion is that children with more deep seated mental health difficulties might need to spend more time in the NG, or receive greater family support. These insecure children might be threatened in the modern classroom and need a slower pace of activities, with attention given to introducing tasks. In the mainstream classroom these NG features are not usually replicated and it could be that roots of marginalisation and failure are established at this point. Children who are restless, have poor concentration, are easily distracted and have difficulties in considering the consequences of their actions seem to pose particular challenges for others.

Thus, NGs help a wide range of children and assist in the management of conduct problems like temper tantrums and obedience; they also reduce other anti-social behaviour such as fighting, lying, cheating and stealing.

Views of the parents and teachers

In Cooper's research, adult voices suggested that NGs had a positive impact on relationships between child and parent and on pupil progress. Parents noted progress with children's attitudes to school and work and became more optimistic about their children's future. They shifted blame away from themselves and the child. Like teachers, the vast majority of parents had positive views about NGs.

Pupils' views

The research findings here are particularly relevant to the present discussion, though young pupils were recognised as being difficult to interview. Children loved both the NG and the mainstream class, so that school was viewed as a positive place to be. They liked increased opportunities to play and this was doubtless because such activities were more in keeping with the level of the pupils. Routines and clear expectations were valued, so that a simpler regime was what was needed. They liked calmness and quietness and simple routine and the interactive style of the staff helped them to engage with tasks. The importance of the NG staff and relationships between them for acquiring skills was noted. Appropriate behaviour was demonstrated so that pupils had the opportunity to observe and practise this in an accepting environment. Also, children took great pride in ownership of the NG and this was helped by involving them in selecting the group name.

To conclude, Cooper's research suggests that NGs promote the social/emotional and educational progress of pupils with a wide range of problems. However, not all pupils generalise the improvements they make in the NG to their mainstream classroom and curriculum adaptations and changes are required. Teachers, pupils and parents value NGs highly and they are seen to impact positively on the mainstream school. However, despite their popularity with school staff, parents and pupils, there are sustainability concerns in small schools and other problems linked to resources.

Some key issues and conclusions

1. Schools need to own these interventions and retain the link between NGs and the whole-school ethos in an interactive system. NGs need to be part of the notion of the inclusive or 'nurturing

school' so that people are valued, understood and respected as unique individuals. Such shared values provide a model of co-operation and active school involvement for children and families. Senior management need to support the NG and clarify its role as an agent of change and training to create a positive, constructive and developmental approach to emotional and behaviour difficulties. It is only through careful use of groups within schools that the dangers of segregation can be avoided. Our dilemma of separating for inclusion can be understood in these terms.

2. The differential effectiveness of NGs for particular pupils requires classroom organisation, which reflects the pace and organisation of the NG on a permanent basis. Certain aspects of the early years' curriculum: literacy and numeracy strategies and classroom organisation must be questioned. Literacy and numeracy activities might need to be spread across the day in shorter sessions. Pupils with additional learning or behavioural needs can require a slower pace, increased structure and more repetition, in order to learn effectively. Some useful NG approaches include areas for breakfast, home or books, free writing, computers, water tray, café or shop, dressing up and a central work base. Schools could incorporate these arrangements in their planning for more vulnerable pupils.

3. Whilst it is not easy to obtain young children's views, we need to increase our efforts to listen to pupils regarding NGs. In the Doncaster NG, some additional piloting of the interview schedule with pupils and actually involving them in the design of the questions would have helped. Pupils taking adults round a group and telling them how it works, in their own words, would have been useful. The initial plan for children to see the video recording afterwards helped them value participation and gained co-operation and involvement. Discussion of video recordings of NG activities with pupils is a useful way of teaching skills and for listening to them. Other methods can be used to help pupils understand questions: alternatives can be represented in visual form and a pointing response used to indicate preferences.

4. NGs offer a graded and manageable way to develop social and emotional skills generally. Whilst circle time can assist with skills such as turn taking, expressing feelings and making positive comments about others, many pupils find this difficult in a large classroom because they may have to wait for excessive amounts of time for their turn. The active child or kinaesthetic learner needs a simpler and more immediate approach. Working in pairs or small groups is a good alternative in a NG or classroom setting. The recognition of pupil learning style is important in the way questions are put to pupils. If a range of visual or pictorial clues accompany simplified and concrete adult language, some ways forward are possible. Some questions in the investigation might more fruitfully have been presented in pairs or smaller groups. In response to the question 'At what age can we listen to the views of young children?' it clearly depends on a range of factors, including areas of ability and the way in which questions are asked. It is dangerous to assume that children are developmentally incapable or insufficiently informed to give views on appropriate approaches to learning or behaviour (see also Gamman in Chapter 10).

5. Assumptions about pupil and parent competence can also be dangerous and damaging. Viewing a child as having some attachment pathology, certainly with the more active group of pupils, can be inaccurate and lead to negative self-fulfilling prophecies for parents and pupils, such as alienation or exclusion. Physical or structural factors often underlie these difficulties. The nurturing and inclusive school will listen to the voices of both pupils and parents who are at risk of being marginalised. Steps could be taken to empower and involve parents in these groups to avoid the undermining and de-skilling danger that the NG teacher is seen as the expert responsible for any improvements children make.

6. Clear criteria are needed for judging readiness for leaving such provision and subsequent pupil support methods. Rebecca Doyle's (2002) Reintegration Readiness scales help to identify skills required for re-integration such as self-control, social and self-awareness, achievement and approach to tasks are covered.

Overall target levels for gradual re-integration can be established for coping in the classroom by involving the class teacher. Above all, the appropriate social processes need to be in place to ensure that the group functions for the benefit of its pupils.

7. Whilst research indicates that NGs are an effective intervention, we need to be aware of the current political agenda which demands that schools raise achievement, but does not promote inclusion. Schools are concerned about pupils missing curriculum opportunities as this will reflect on their results. For some, social goals are paramount and need addressing. Whilst there are dangers of segregating those who interfere with the learning of others, we need to create a balanced group and EPs are well placed to support the development of such groups in the capacity of 'critical friend'. Such provision might most usefully be seen as a flexible 'School Action' intervention under the SEN Code of Practice (2001), with the EP having a role in assisting the school to decide who might enter the group and by contributing to discussions about reintegration.

8. Sustainable provision is required and given current funding approaches with less central LEA financial support being available, other mechanisms are required to support these ventures. Nevertheless, LEAs need to develop coherent plans and such interventions should be included in Behaviour Support and LEA Development Plans. Such plans would be usefully supplemented by the provision of appropriate operational guidelines for such groups.

9. We need to recognise that teacher and school culture factors often operate negatively and lead towards segregation, particularly for those with EBD. An appropriately resourced and real NG can make positive gains, especially if it is fully integrated within a supportive neighbourhood school, with the child remaining part of his or her peer group and community. Elements of NG practice can be incorporated in general classroom organisation and activities but where differences are seen as unacceptable, segregated or PRU provision will probably remain. Clearly, professionals need to seek out the voice of the child, including that of the youngest child to develop inclusive, effective and responsive services for children.

7

Including me in: Can we learn from the voice of disabled children?

Katie Clarke and Keith Venables

Introduction

What are you here for? To help me out or just to rub it in? (disabled child in Special School, South Yorkshire (England), 1999 to one of the authors.)

Communication is at the centre of our lives. It is something we need to do in order to express our identity as individual human beings, to have relationships with others, to take our place as citizens in the society in which we live. (J. Morris in Preface to Marchant and Gordon, 2001 p 4)

Disabled people and especially disabled children are seen as on the margins of society. Rieser and Peasley (2002) argue that the negative social constructions of disabled people act as a barrier to life's opportunities. Disabled people are 'in need of charity', odd and freaks or even downright dangerous. These constructions may lead to the conclusion that disabled children can make little contribution to society or even to managing their own lives.

Such views of disability set a framework within which the roles of all school staff such as teachers, school managers and learning support staff, as well as professionals like health visitors and educational psychologists who support children and schools, are played out. This chapter, written by the mother of a disabled daughter and by an educational psychologist with professional experience of working with children with 'severe learning disabilities,' sets out to clarify how such children and young people with high level support needs can be enabled to express their voice and be listened to. It explores the role of professionals as allies in this process and illustrates some of the issues through the example of those important professionals, educational psychologists (EPs), questioning whether sometimes EPs keep children on the margins and outside the circle. We argue that there is much to learn from disabled children, if only we listen.

A meeting of allies?

Following the 1981 Education Act (England and Wales), which brought in the idea that some children have special educational needs, a group of parents established 'Network 81' as 'a national network of parents working towards properly resourced inclusive education for children with special educational needs'. At the turn of the millennium, we were keynote speakers at 'Network 81' Annual Conferences. Katie spoke about the struggle to get an included place for her disabled daughter in a mainstream school and Keith spoke about what he thought parents have a right to expect from professionals within the Local Education Authority (LEA).

A year later we found ourselves in the same LEA in the north of England, as parent and as educational psychologist, encouraging service providers to listen to the voice of disabled children and to their parents. We decided that it might be useful to set out some kind of guidance for how education professionals could help parents and their disabled children create change though having a voice.

Katie's daughter – Nadia – had a bad start accessing education and although the primary school has been a positive experience, there have been many issues about finding the right level of expertise in educating a child with complex needs. This is becoming more apparent as Nadia goes through transition to high school. The need for skilled staff and more training is evident: without this she will struggle to access the curriculum and face barriers to learning. Katie did not believe that the educational psychologists in Nadia's family's life had made a positive difference: rather her impression was that some had offered supposedly neutral assessment information and others had played no part at all. We thought that some kind of discussion of what disabled children and their families need would be useful; and that it might clarify the role of professionals in the process.

This book seeks to 'challenge theories and practices that serve to marginalise children' and is intended to contribute to the debate on inclusion. It explores the current international educational context, drawing out key themes and intentions, especially to promote 'inclusion' and to 'listen to the voice of the child'. Further, it questions to the extent to which these lofty aims are being achieved and seeks a useful way of looking at the underlying issues. It examines good practice about listening to and learning from the voices of children and young people with high level support needs and considers the role of allies in helping to do this. In our chapter we illustrate these issues and also discuss whether there can be a social model of educational psychology.

Emerging themes
In 1994 The United Nations Educational, Scientific and Cultural Organisation (UNESCO) met and issued the *Salamanca Statement*, asserting a right for the world's children to be included in mainstream education and setting tasks for governments to understand, support and develop this right. In the UK in 1997, after considerable lobbying from parents' groups, groups of disabled people, education professionals and human rights campaigners, David Blunkett, Secretary of State for Education and Employment (DfEE) for the new Labour government, committed the government to educational inclusion

> The education of children with special needs is a key challenge for the nation. It is vital to the creation of a fully inclusive society, a society in which all members see themselves as valued for the contribution they make. We owe all children – whatever their particular needs and circumstances – the opportunity to develop to their full potential, to contribute economically, and to play a full part as active citizens. (DfEE, *Excellence for All Children*, 1997 (Introduction)

He continued

...the special educational needs of most children can be met effectively in mainstream schools.

Many people welcomed these statements, suggesting as they did that the needs of all children, including those with special needs, were to be recognised and their contribution welcomed. Further, they implied that special schools were to be phased out, supporting the view that they isolate disabled children educationally and socially, emphasising their deficits and differentness rather than their potential and commonality with all children.

Many of us in the inclusion lobby were disappointed when, the following year, the DfEE backtracked on the closure of special schools in their *Meeting Special Educational Needs: a programme of action*

For some, a mainstream placement may not be right, or not right just yet. (DfEE, 1998 p 23)

However, although we are confident that properly thought out and resourced local community schools would be best able to meet the educational needs of all children and allow them access to improved opportunities in life, this is not the only issue. We argue that inclusion is more fundamental than a debate between mainstream and special schools. An education system should serve the needs of the society and its citizens, including all of its children, and this requires flexibility and diversity. However, overcoming the barriers to developing the potential of disabled children requires some fundamental principles to be in place.

Excellence for Children (DfEE, 1997) set off a rich and valuable debate in England and Wales about educational opportunities and provision but this has been a debate full of contradictions. For example, the subsequent Special Educational Needs and Disability Rights Act (SENDA, 2001) issued a Code of Practice about how to deal with the individual needs of 'children with special educational needs'. This draws on and extends the approach outlined in the Warnock Report (1978) which laid the basis for the 1981 or 'special educational needs' Education Act. Here again the focus is on within child deficits and offers a range of interventions to address individual children's special needs, up to and including a statement of special needs, issued by the LEA.

Interestingly, SENDA 2001 also embraces the inclusion agenda and expects schools, supported by the LEA, to make reasonable adjustments to allow them to become more able to accommodate diversity and a range of needs. This Act directs its focus on within child issues, outlining a way to help them overcome their personal deficits, while recognising that the way schools are organised needs to be changed to accommodate a wider range of children's needs.

A similar and significant contradiction is that schools are under considerable pressure to achieve a good reputation with high examination and key stage test results. Parents are more likely to choose high reputation schools for their children and this brings in important funding. Disabled children and those with special needs could bring the overall results down and this may act as a disincentive to other parents. Therefore, schools may not welcome disabled children and this is a pressure against inclusion. Even if students with special educational needs attract additional funding through money delegated to the school or by being given funds as part of a statement of special educational needs, there is still a problem. Such children only attract funding if they have identifiable special needs and need help to prevent them from failing. When they begin to succeed, the funding is no longer needed and is withdrawn. This offers a perverse incentive, possibly discouraging schools from reporting success.

No wonder Mary Warnock, in *What a disaster we created* (Gold, 2003) says that she is critical of the Special Needs Act 1981 she inspired; 'It changed attitudes to disability but introduced a system that, instead of focusing on children's needs, became a financial battleground.' SENDA 2001 resources schools for making reasonable adjustments but can take funding away for achieving success with individual students.

The *Salamanca Statement* encourages the participation of all children in mainstream schooling yet in England and Wales disabled children are both invited into and rejected from such schools. A philosophy that draws upon the notion that problems are within the child (sometimes called the child deficit or medical model) sits alongside a philosophy which expects schools to make reasonable adjustments which accommodate a wider range of children and their needs. At the same time the majority of funding to most schools is likely to come through high examination results and disabled children rarely contribute to these results.

There should be a way of understanding and valuing the contribution disabled children can make which is central to education and schooling in England and Wales. We argue that this social model of disability is more helpful and we will expand on it later in the chapter. The social model attempts to bring disabled children back in from the margins.

A bit of common sense

In November 2002, the Audit Commission in its report *SEN: A mainstream issue* brought considerable clarity to the debate. Having researched the statementing process which emerged from the 1981 Education Act, it concluded that a radical rethink of all special needs was necessary. Good education and sound inclusion could be seen in terms of four crucial areas: presence, acceptance, participation and achievement.

The Audit Commission suggested that for a school or setting to be truly inclusive, all four conditions should apply to all children attending, regardless of their abilities and disabilities and other factors such as their ethnic origin, social class or gender. It is not sufficient for disabled children just to be present in the school, they need to be accepted by their peers and all school staff, they need to participate in all of the school's activities and they need to reach good levels of attainment in their work and behaviour.

In this Chapter we are not just critical of theories and practices which marginalise children but we seek new practices and conceptualisations which bring children into the circle.

It could be argued that the purpose of education is to enable all children to fulfil their potential and thus be inclusive in the way described by the Audit Commission. A definition of inclusion which contains these four elements would be valuable. Although a decade ago the term inclusion was rarely used, today the UK Government Inspectors of Schools for England and Wales feel that its clear definition is important enough to present in guidance to schools.

An educationally inclusive school is one in which the teaching and learning, achievements and attitudes and well-being of every young person matters. Effective schools are educationally inclusive schools. This shows, not only in their performance, but also in their ethos and their willingness to offer new opportunities to pupils who may have experienced previous difficulties. The most effective schools do not take educational inclusion for granted. They constantly monitor and evaluate the progress each pupil makes. They identify any pupils who may be missing out, difficult to engage, or feeling in some way apart from what the school seeks to provide. (Ofsted, 2000 p 2)

Inclusion refers to the opportunity for persons with a disability to participate fully in the educational, employment, consumer, recreational, community and domestic activities that typify everyday society. (Inclusion International, 1996, as quoted in Rieser and Peasley, 2002)

These definitions emphasise not only the presence, acceptance, participation and achievement of children in schools but also the importance of access to life's opportunities of leisure and employment. The second definition arises from within the disability rights movement.

Disabled people lead the way

This movement offers the richest insights into what needs to change in the educational system and this can happen. In *Disability Equality in the Classroom: a human rights issue*, Rieser and Mason (1990), two disabled activists and academics, argue that the recognition of the needs of disabled people is a struggle which must be led by disabled people themselves. In what is a partly a practical handbook for teachers, they suggest changes in school curriculum, organisation and accessibility such as recommending that the discussion of images of disabled people in stories and the media should be part of the curriculum. However, perhaps more significant is their insistence that changes of the kind later called for by the *Salamanca Statement* have to be fought for; they will not just happen. Further, they propose a way of looking at the inclusion of disabled people which brings considerable clarity – the social model.

Medical model or social model?

The term *disabled*, with its negative connotations, implies that children with, for example, cerebral palsy are themselves simply disabled. We should maybe banish the use of this term and prefer notions that emanate from the 1981 Education Act. This discourages the use of labels such as disabled and encourages a focus on the provision to address children's needs. However, this dilemma begins to be resolved if we examine the key concept of this chapter, which is that there is an opposition between the medical and the social model of disability. Without this understanding, our ability to take meaningful action is limited.

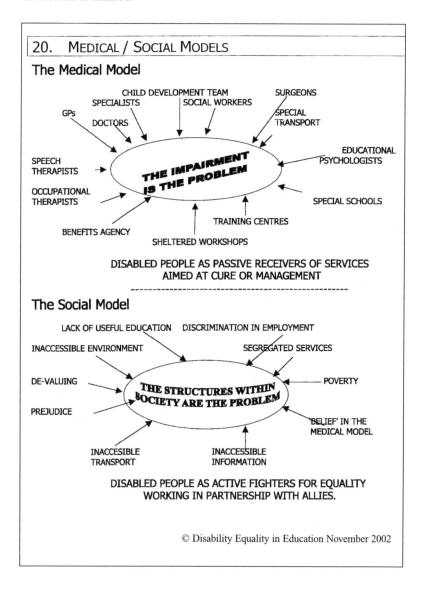

20. MEDICAL / SOCIAL MODELS

The Medical Model

CHILD DEVELOPMENT TEAM
SPECIALISTS   SOCIAL WORKERS
SURGEONS
GPs
DOCTORS
SPECIAL TRANSPORT
SPEECH THERAPISTS
EDUCATIONAL PSYCHOLOGISTS
THE IMPAIRMENT IS THE PROBLEM
OCCUPATIONAL THERAPISTS
SPECIAL SCHOOLS
BENEFITS AGENCY
TRAINING CENTRES
SHELTERED WORKSHOPS

DISABLED PEOPLE AS PASSIVE RECEIVERS OF SERVICES
AIMED AT CURE OR MANAGEMENT

The Social Model

LACK OF USEFUL EDUCATION   DISCRIMINATION IN EMPLOYMENT
INACCESSIBLE ENVIRONMENT
SEGREGATED SERVICES
DE-VALUING
THE STRUCTURES WITHIN SOCIETY ARE THE PROBLEM
POVERTY
PREJUDICE
BELIEF' IN THE MEDICAL MODEL
INACCESIBLE TRANSPORT
INACCESSIBLE INFORMATION

DISABLED PEOPLE AS ACTIVE FIGHTERS FOR EQUALITY
WORKING IN PARTNERSHIP WITH ALLIES.

© Disability Equality in Education November 2002

The medical model sees the child as the centre of the difficulty and in need of adjustment. The social model draws an important distinction between an individual's specific impairment (e.g. a physical, sensory or cognitive impairment) and the existence and effects of disabling barriers. The focus for change is on these disabling barriers, which include: prejudice, discrimination, negative attitudes, denial of opportunities, and lack of support, including support to express views and to be listened to. This is why we have not referred to children with disabilities (this implies that children carry barriers around with them) but refer to disabled children. Equally, we have not referred to children with special educational needs, nor does the term SEN children make sense. The medical model would describe SEN as within the child; whereas the social model might seek ways to enrich the school so that it can accommodate a diversity of students' needs (Ofsted definition of inclusion, (*op cit*).

For the social model, the key task is to learn how to remove these barriers. Fundamental to moving these barriers is the need to develop a powerful respect for the views of disabled children and to learn how to appreciate them.

Rieser and Peasley (2002), speaking from within the disabled peoples' rights movement, argue that the medical model usually focuses

> ... on the impairment... rather than the needs of the person. The power to change us seems to lie with the medical and associated professions, with their talk of cures, normalisation and science. Often our lives are handed over to them.
>
> Other people's assessments of us, usually by non-disabled professionals, are used to determine where we go to school, what support we get and what type of education; where we live, whether or not we can work and what kind of work we do and indeed whether we are born at all, or even allowed to procreate. Similar control is exercised over us by the design of the built environment presenting us with many barriers, therefore making it difficult or impossible for our needs to be met and curtailing our life chances. (Rieser and Peasley (2002, p 41)

We would argue that there is nothing as practical as a good idea and the social model of disability is a good idea. It allows an approach that is respectful to the essential humanity of all children and encourages the search for solutions to overcome barriers and discover potential.

We are of the view that the position of disabled people and the discrimination against us are socially created. This has little do with our impairments. As a disabled person you are made to feel it is your own fault that you are different. ...Through fear, ignorance and prejudice, barriers and discriminatory practices develop which disable us. The understanding of the process of disablement allows disabled people to feel good about themselves and empowers us to fight for our human rights. ... Our fight for the inclusion of all children, however, 'severely' disabled, in one mainstream, education system, will not make sense unless the difference in 'social' and 'medical' model of disability is understood. (Rieser and Peasley (*op cit.* pp 42-43)

It is possible to argue that, at its best, SENDA 2001 is an expression of the social model of disability, since it seeks to remove barriers to presence, acceptance, participation and achievement of disabled children by emphasising reasonable adjustments to existing schools. It is also possible to argue that, at its worst, the special needs legislation that has come from the 1978 Warnock Report is an expression of the medical model; it focuses in on the child and their special needs.

What is an ally?

An ally is somebody who understands that his or her role is to support somebody else's struggle. Inherent in this approach is the notion that human rights are crucial and that a campaign to achieve them is necessary. The *Salamanca Statement* outlines those rights and the social model insists that disabled people and their allies need to get together to achieve those rights. This is very different to some professional views; such professionals would know best and give themselves the right to make decisions on behalf of the disabled person and their family.

It can be argued that one of the consequences of Warnock's Report was a special needs industry full of experts, statementing officers, health professionals, educational psychologists, specialist teachers, more recently special needs co-ordinators (SENCOs), advisory groups, 'SEN' lawyers and so on. However, expertise is not neutral. Murray and Penman (2000) give many accounts of how experts take on the right to make decisions for – and not with – children and their families.

The social model is a challenge to professionals; it asks them to be allies, sharing decision making and finding ways to bring down the barriers. It asks for support to challenge prejudice and negative attitudes and to support means of letting disabled children and their families find their own voice.

Allies reject the view that those who appear not to be able to speak have nothing to say. Struggling to support disabled children with high level support needs find a *voice*, speak out and influence decisions is a challenge worth accepting.

Participation and communication

Full participation is not just a theme which has arisen within education. In 1989 in England and Wales, the Children Act (1989) asserted that, 'the rights of the child are paramount' and in 2000, the Department of Health *Framework for the Assessment of Children in Need and their Families* emphasised the importance of consulting meaningfully with all children; it gives explicit guidance on involving disabled children in assessment processes.

The Quality Protects programme for England prioritises

> ...listening to the views of children, young people and their families and drawing on their experience to help them plan and deliver services and strengthen the voice of children in their day-to-day settings with a view to improving safety. (Kahn and Russell, 1999)

The Special Needs and Disability Rights Act 2001 (DfES, 2001) promotes the 'active partnership between children, their parents, schools, Local Education Authorities, and health and social services, including the right of children to be heard in the assessment of their educational needs.'

However, ten years after the Children Act, it could still be stated that

> ...disabled children and young people are rarely consulted or involved in decisions about their care... workers do not feel they have the necessary skills or experience to communicate with them. (Joseph Rowntree Foundation, 1999, p 3)

And this is important as real participation is crucial. Can we listen to and learn from the voice of disabled children and their families? Can we learn to listen and hear?

> Communication is at the centre of our lives. It is something we need to do in order to express our identity as individual human beings, to have relationships with others, to take our place as citizens in the society in which we live. (Morris, 2001, p 4)

This is a profound statement; it implies that education generally would benefit from practices in which allies have the skills to enable disabled children to express their voice.

Every child matters

Disabled children have the same needs as all children. The Irish Society for the Prevention of Cruelty to Children asks, 'What do children need?' They suggest that all children need 'love, praise, physical care, routines, stimulation, talking, independence and respect'. They add 'parents and carers matter, too!'

For anyone wishing to contribute positively to helping children and their parents and carers get what they need, close attention to these basic principles is suggested. If we are not able to communicate with disabled children we are helping deny them the essence of what it is to be human and the gift of their voice.

Barbara Herts (2001) suggests some guiding principles for effective participation. These are:

- to ensure that children, young people and their families are not discriminated against and prevented from participating effectively on the grounds of race, culture, disability, age, ethnic origin or language

- to ensure inclusion of disabled children and support, where necessary, for carers and parents

- to make sure consultation is accessible through the use of Braille, tape or signers

- to ensure venues have disabled access and there is ease of access to other parts of the building

- to provide adult support for younger children and young people who want it

- to use plain language and make sure language is appropriate to the age and maturity of the child

- to make use of films, CD ROMs and electronic methods that are familiar and fun to the child and young person

- that if the work is adult-initiated then to be honest about this

- to develop children's skills by recognising that participation helps in developing skills useful for debate, communication, negotiation, prioritisation and decision-making

- to develop the skills of staff

- to develop the skills of parents and carers

- to give feedback and ensure that there are speedy mechanisms for updating those who take part and be prepared to be flexible and creative and last but not least, make life enjoyable (Herts, 2001, p 3)

This should allow a set of shared values to evolve and encourage the development of frameworks and examples of good practice. It sets out some key tasks for allies.

Learning to listen

Bell (2002) reminds us of the importance of active listening. He comments that when we exchange social meaning, we define others and ourselves in society, especially those with whom we spend our lives.

> Good listening has important value and can be learnt, and improved, to yield enormous benefits. The process is called 'active listening. It takes effort, but everyone can and should learn to do it.' (Bell, B. p 3)

Another important area is the opportunity for disabled children to have role models such as other young people, disabled adults, and disabled professionals, who show what can be done. Disabled children also need to look to their own parents for advice and support and as perhaps the most significant role models in their lives.

Communication is never easy

For many parents, communicating with their own children is not a simple or even natural process. When a family have a newborn disabled child it is usual for them to have had little contact with anyone disabled. It is rare that a parent would have developed or even had the opportunity to communicate with a disabled adult. Their own fears, prejudices and lack of understanding of the world of disability will play a significant part in how they relate to their own child. How the parent feels about their child will not only have an effect on how they communicate with their disabled child but also huge implications on how the child will grow and develop cognitively and emotionally.

Parents, therefore, need to understand that their disabled child has an equal right to have a *voice* and that much of their parenting skills need to go on developing their child's potential. Parents need to help their children to communicate their feelings, to make choices, to have relationships and to be included. A child who does not communicate cannot be fully included. Parents need to quickly learn these important skills. For example, these may include using Yes/No choices, practical objects of reference, symbols and signs. The development of their own self-esteem and confidence as parents of a disabled child is also crucial.

LEAs can play a part in developing and generalising good practice. This can take the form of working in teams with the parents and child as equal partners. These teams could be guided by an occupational therapist helping to find appropriate seating and positioning of a child. Access is a major issue for many children and there is a need for correct switches, joysticks and other aids essential for the child to communicate. A high expectation of children and young people through ordinary curriculum activity is essential. However, the LEA needs to be committed to ensure that all staff, including learning and personal support assistants, are adequately trained in IT and alternative means of communication. There are added financial implications for resource time, individual support teachers and funding to provide the necessary technology for the child to communicate.

Marchant and Gordon (2001) suggest that the facilitation of communication needs solid planning and preparation, using the appropriate approaches and writing up and giving feedback and review.

In particular, they advocate finding out how the child usually communicates, giving careful thought to your initial approach, developing a range of communication resources, having a wide and open definition of communication, making approaches to the young person responsive and individualised, using language carefully, being non-directive and taking time, giving the young person time to expand a message before going on to the next open question, responding respectively to young people's use of communication and being careful not to be distracted by the method of communication. Finally, they suggest we ensure using a balance between what the child said or signed or communicated directly and what he or she actually did, and using checking means to ensure that what you think you understood was what was actually communicated.

High technology, such as the Internet, can have a liberating potential. The authors both communicate with particular friends, some of whom have significant impairments, via the Internet. These friends cannot use speech to communicate but can pass greetings over many miles through the Internet.

An electronic communication aid can be the child's only access to the ability to express thoughts and feelings. This can take years to learn to use and requires skills from parents and those working with the child to motivate and encourage use within school, home and the community. This aid can be the path to participation in activities, having friendships and access to the school curriculum.

Can educational psychologists be allies?

We now turn to the role that educational psychologists (EPs) might play as allies in supporting the move of disabled children from the margins to the centre. Farrell (2004) notes that teachers in different countries see EPs having 'a major responsibility for assessing and re-commending resources for pupils who are experiencing difficulties with learning and behaviour.' EPs are seen as able to make recom-mendations for segregated provision or for inclusive arrangements. The teachers argued that by working within the local authority and with schools, EPs can help to develop more inclusive policies and practices which affect the education of all children.

Farrell explores how the role of an educational psychologist is con-structed. He asks to what extent EPs operate within the medical or the social model and whether EPs can act as allies. Certainly, the DfEE Report on the future of Educational Psychology Services (2000) ex-plicitly encourages the development of an inclusive perspective with-in the role of EP Services. However, examination of the standard text-books which inform the first degree in psychology adopt a within-person model, where explanations about behaviour and learning can be made by focusing on the individual. Further, despite serious questions about the scientific validity of Intelligence Quotient (IQ) testing, this approach is still widely used. Statements of special educational needs often includes advice from EPs which uses cognitive testing and IQ test results to describe the child. Rarely do EPs include advice about bringing down barriers in their reports; instead, they tend to focus on the abilities and potential that can be seen within the child.

Although this academic grounding may shape the way EPs undertake their work, there are a number of expectations within the EPs' professional role which make the promotion of inclusion problematic in terms of supporting disabled students return back from the margins. An EP's typical workload is made up of referrals from a school. A teacher or SENCO who refers the child will see that child as possessing a number of difficulties implicitly focused on within-the-child problems. There is, therefore, an expectation that the educational psychologist will see the child, either in the classroom, or in a separate room, undertake some individual work and report back to the school. Discussion with school staff is likely to be about gathering more information to help explain the child's problems. Throughout this process, the school and its teachers may have a vested interest in arriving at explanations about the problem which are placed firmly within the child. 'It's not our fault, we do our best. Please explain this child to me.' This is the medical model in operation.

On the other hand, the EP could operate the social model. This would begin with discovering what barriers there are to the child's learning or sense of well-being and go on to working co-operatively with the child and with key adults in that child's life to bring down those barriers. It might be that the curriculum needs more differentiation, or that the teacher needs to have better skills appropriate to the diversity of children in the class. Further, it is possible that friendships or relationships with parents and carers might be developed more positively.

The educational psychologist needs to have a range of skills in these relationships, developing the trust and confidence of teachers so that they are willing to change their teaching and learning strategies, enabling various adults to work together more effectively: discussing with parents, school management and local authority staff where significant resources are needed and, crucially, supporting the child's own ability to understand, articulate and manage their own situation.

The EP who adopts the social model will require the credibility and skills to know

> how to improve the learning and teaching environment for the child within the mainstream school – indeed, how to make his or her education more inclusive from the point of view of presence, acceptance, participation and achievement, the four aspects of inclusion. (Farrell *et al*, 2004)

It is interesting that the recent British Psychological Society outline of a new three year course for training Educational Psychologists does not even mention the debate about the medical and social models, although this is a significant debate that has emerged from within the disability rights movement.

This certainly leaves open the possibility of educational psychologists learning how to empower all of those concerned with addressing learning needs and promoting inclusion. It is possible that EPs might become allies not simply professional commentators, and there is certainly a debate to be had about theory and practice.

Conclusion

At the heart of this chapter is the notion that constructions of disability are a political matter. Disabled children are at the margins when it is assumed that they possess a deficit (the medical model). They can be in the mainstream when their voice is heard and when their allies help bring down the barriers to their expression, inclusion and full rights (social model).

Although this approach is embodied in the *Salamanca Statement* and UK government policy, there is a still a long way to go. There are exciting tasks ahead and we hope we have outlined some of them. In particular, these authors believe there is a great deal to learn when we to listen to disabled children, and that we will all benefit from what we hear.

Finally, Katie and Keith met in a spirit of optimism at the turn of the millennium, believing that we could be allies and help to bring about changes. This is still firmly our belief.

8

Talking and listening to children diagnosed with ADHD and taking psychostimulants

Tiny Arora and Lynne Mackey

It's like a computer without the hard drive – it won't work will it.

This chapter is about children who take tablets to make them behave better. We meet them in our daily work. They are unable to sit still for long. Their attention wanders. They do unexpected and sometimes harmful acts without thinking. Parents and teachers worry about such children and feel they should be able to behave better. Perhaps they could, given the right environment, consistency, clear communication, sufficient help or attention, or, quite simply, more time to mature. However, if concerned parents can convince their GP, the child is referred to a specialist, often a paediatrician. Medical specialists tend to provide medical answers to referred problems and so there is a high possibility the child, usually a boy is diagnosed as having ADHD and prescribed medication to make him behave.

For the past fifty years practitioners working with children have been challenged by cognitive and behavioural problems categorised as disorders of attention, impulsivity and hyperactivity, in short ADHD (Attention Deficit Hyperactivity Disorder). Despite the effects of ADHD being intensely felt in the social environment of the classroom, the expertise of educators and the experience of pupils are marginalised as the medical profession dominates research, diagnosis and treatment. Few researchers have asked what the process of diagnosis and prescription feels like from the point of view of the children concerned. In reporting on the interviews Lynne undertook with children diagnosed as having ADHD and subsequently taking medication, our main aim is to let the adults hear what the children had to say. We do not claim to write on the children's behalf, as they may not interpret the issues as we do. What we do is to comment on what we think are important issues arising from the talks with the children, often quoting their words verbatim for better understanding and impact. Like others in this book, we consider it a right for children not only to be individual but also to feel involved in decisions that have a big influence on how they see themselves and on how others will see them. As such, there are major implications for support services and schools, which we shall discuss in our conclusions. But first there is a need to fully understand the background to the processes described above.

Does ADHD exist?

...the discovery of ADHD represents not so much an unveiling of a condition that has been waiting to be discovered, but rather a convergence of complex social, political, economic, medical and psychological factors coming together at the right time. (Armstrong, 1995, p 8)

Despite the large and growing body of research (see for instance, Goldstein and Goldstein, 1998; Root and Reswick, 2003), the diagnosis of ADHD lacks a critical component. It does not inform us about the causes. There is no common agreement about how to assess and treat it. If we take Armstrong's argument above we could conclude that it only exists as a convenient label for a number of behaviours which are difficult to manage. We do know that an increasing number of young people, mostly in mainstream schools, are diagnosed as having ADHD and are taking medication in connection with it. It has been suggested that this increase is due to parents seeking medical, within-child based explanations for children's behaviour difficulties (Maras *et al.* 2002), but equally this could not have happened without cooperation from the medical profession.

We contend that rather than focus on the label, it is much more meaningful to try to determine what the child's strengths and weaknesses are, what is in the environment which may help or hinder learning and behaviour and, in partnership with the child and significant others, to remove barriers.

Diagnostic Procedures

In the UK, a range of professionals are involved with the identification and management of ADHD, although not every child or parent has contact with all of them. It is common for the final diagnosis to be made by a paediatrician. There is no physical test for ADHD. As is the case for most psychiatric disorders, the diagnosis is made almost exclusively on the basis of a history obtained from parents or other family members, teachers and the child concerned (Zametkin and Ernst, 1999). It is based purely on personal perspectives. Parents of children with an ADHD diagnosis are able to apply for an Attendance Allowance which provides additional financial support. In cases of genuine need this is of real help, but in some instances parents' motivation to seek a diagnosis may be influenced by monetary factors and there is a suspicion that financial benefit rather than the needs of the child can become the main priority.

Questions need be asked about which sectors of society receive diagnosis and treatment. A statistical review of medication in Adelaide, Australia showed a higher prescription rate in areas of lower income and unemployment (Prosser, 1999). It also revealed that children from middle to higher income families were more likely to be described as having the inattentive rather than hyperactive subtype. The issue here is whether such variations in diagnostic practice reflect genuine differences in incidence. Are there really more children with ADHD in lower income and employment groups or are we dealing with social and contextual factors such as child rearing, adverse environments at home or at school and cultural expectations?

Management of ADHD

Many authors argue that children who have difficulties with attention, impulsivity and hyperactivity benefit from a variety of approaches (British Psychological Society 1996; Root and Reswick, 2003). Behaviour modification programmes, counselling, parent training, provision of structure and classroom support and curriculum modifications should be used before medication is begun and continued whilst it is in place. Medication is often described as providing a 'window of opportunity' to allow other strategies to be more effective (Kewley, 1999). It can improve the child's concentration and focusing in the short term but it is often the other strategies which are seen as having the potential to bring about long term change.

Medication

We have noted that an ADHD diagnosis depends upon a number of complex factors including chance. However, once a diagnosis has been given the likelihood of medication is very high. Medicating children has been the centre of considerable controversy and media interest. Whilst many are fearful of the consequences of the prescription of stimulant medication for children, there are those who will bear witness to the dramatic improvements in the lives of children treated.

Ritalin (Methylphenidate Hydrochloride) is the most common drug used in the United Kingdom, recently being prescribed in slow release form Concerta. Using brain imaging, scientists have shown that brain dopamine levels increase significantly approximately 60 minutes after ingesting Ritalin. It is also thought to suppress the firing of neurons not normally associated with task performance thus allowing the brain to transmit a clearer signal (Volkow, 2001).

Some parent support groups have been assisted financially by pharmaceutical companies (Merritt, 1995), adding to the unease felt about financial incentives for parents to have their children diagnosed as having ADHD. Therefore, both parents and drug companies can clearly benefit financially from such a diagnosis.

The length of time a child is prescribed medication varies but it can be long term unless there are contra-indications at an early stage. Side effects whilst taking the drugs can include appetite suppression, headaches or abdominal pain, sleep difficulties and tics. There could also be a rebound effect when the difficulties increase as soon as the drug's effect wears off. A worrying development is that some children are prescribed other drugs to take alongside Ritalin. One such drug is Risperdol, used in the treatment of adult schizophrenia, and never formally trialled on children.

Concern has been expressed that there is a market for selling on the freely prescribed drugs (Merritt, 1995), whilst recent focus group interviews in New South Wales suggest that teenagers felt it to be quite normal to share their prescribed drugs including Ritalin with other young people. They tended not to warn their peers of the possible side effects or danger as they assumed that prescription drugs were safer than illegal ones (NSW Commission for Children and Young People, 2001).

Views of the child with ADHD

Cooper and Shea (1998) carried out the first major study on students' perceptions of ADHD. The authors noted that students have been encouraged to think about their condition in biological terms. They argued for a more balanced view of ADHD as a biological, psychological and social condition. They felt that not only would it give children a broader view of what influenced ADHD but would have a positive effect on their self-identity, self-control and their ability to make choices about how they responded in different environments.

This view is strongly supported by Prosser (2004) who examined secondary students' understanding and educational institutions' responses to ADHD in Australia. These pupils saw medication as a way of helping them conform to the expectations of school. However, by the time they reached adolescence they often had long histories of conflict with social institutions. It was at this point that some students began to question the relevance of the ADHD concept itself. Prosser noted that where students struggled was in obtaining the help they needed in the mainstream classroom and frequently they experienced problems building and maintaining relationships with their peers. Similarly, the NSW Commission (NSW Commission for children and young people, 2001) noted that some young people reported that their peers were ostracised for taking Ritalin.

Issues investigated

There are legal, moral and practical reasons for finding out about children's views. The Department of Health has published guidelines on consent for children and young people (2001) but genuine participation of children in making choices about treatment is far less defined.

The main focus of the identification and treatment of ADHD is the child and therefore the value of obtaining young people's perspectives on this process cannot be overestimated. We set out to do this, asking the following questions:

- How do the children view the condition of ADHD?

- What are their experiences before, during and after their diagnosis of ADHD?

- How do they react to and perceive the process of their diagnosis and follow up visits?

- How do they react to and perceive their subsequent pharmaceutical intervention?

- How do they perceive the impact of their medication on their behaviour and learning in school?

A further objective of the study was to develop effective methods for communicating with children and young people about these issues.

The children consulted

Twenty-three children aged between eight and fifteen were interviewed in schools after parental permission was sought. The children were found through two main sources, the local parent support group and educational psychologists. The criteria for selection were a) that the children had received a medical diagnosis of ADHD and b) were taking some form of psychostimulant medication in connection with this. This means that these children had already been exposed to the medical model of ADHD. The sample, theoretically, did not include those who had rejected this model or who had found medication unsuccessful.

The Local Authority from which the children were selected was developing positive multi-disciplinary links and collaborative practice regarding professional responses to ADHD. However tensions continue to exist.

Methods used when talking with the children

Lynne interviewed all the children in school. Care was taken to set the children at ease and engage their interest in a relaxed way. The word ADHD was not mentioned until halfway through the interview to ascertain whether the children would use it spontaneously as a construct or label to explain their behaviour and make sense of their experiences.

The interview schedule was designed as a sequence of short, interesting and varied activities, with the explicit purpose of being suited to children who prefer a practical learning style and have a short attention span. Thus, it consisted of a warm up, a general self-description, a lifeline exercise, an exercise to elicit personal constructs and a 'like me, not like me' activity. Photographs of the hospital and medical personnel involved in the diagnosis were used to help the children recall their earlier experiences more vividly and the wrapping of the medication taken was used as an additional concrete prompt.

Under these circumstances, the children's interviews lasted between 55 and 90 minutes. This showed that they were capable of good concentration and a high level of attention, provided the conditions were right.

The children's story
The condition of ADHD
The responses of the children revealed a strong medical orientation. Some children believed ADHD to be a brain disorder, something missing or not working right in the brain:

> It's cos I've got this thing missing in my brain called dopamine and it's at the back there

> In the brain 'cos the brain's an important part of your body. It's in your nerves (in the brain) but they (children without ADHD) haven't got the same nerves.

Other children believed the disorder could occur by having an accident or injury to the head:

> It's summat what's missing in my brain. My grandma thinks when I got knocked over when I was four and I flew down from near the top right down to the phone she thinks it came out of my brain when I did that.

Other ideas included a heart murmur, something in the blood, a disease that makes you bad or stupid and something in the body that got there by remembering things in the past. A substantial number thought ADHD was the name of the tablets they took:

> He (doctor) talks about ADHD and what time you've got to take them.

A few children constructed ADHD as a behaviour. One of these felt the behaviour (hyperactivity) was physically located in the body:

> It's a behaviour. I think it's what some kids are born to get, what they're born with. I think it's in the body.

Which bit?

> That bit there (points to lump on forehead). You can pull it out...I think it's in loads of places.

A third of children described incidents at home or school arising from difficulties associated with ADHD. The intensity of these difficulties ranged from mild to severe, including a hanging attempt and violent behaviour leading to school exclusion. These children overlapped with those who spontaneously mentioned either their ADHD diagnosis or medication in the lifeline activity. There were a number of children who did not describe behaviour problems or a diagnosis of ADHD, despite acknowledging that they took Ritalin. Many children indicated that they perceive ADHD as a childhood difficulty that they might 'grow out of'.

> I might get better because I get older and then I'll grow out of it. I might grow out of being bad.

Experiences before, during and after the ADHD diagnosis and the children's reactions to this

Most children did not report that gaining a diagnosis and a subsequent label had made a direct impact on their experiences at home or school. Many but not all of the children related stories which illustrated a self-awareness of past and current behavioural difficulties which they felt had already stigmatised them:

> People say stuff, horrible stuff...I get angry. I either swear at them or go over and batter 'em.

This negative self-image is influenced to a considerable degree by significant others: parents, teachers, siblings and peers. The most commonly cited behavioural descriptors with which the children were identified were mad, angry, bad, naughty, and hyper. On further enquiry these words covered a range of behaviours from not listening or paying attention to serious risk taking such as fire setting, jumping off roofs and out of windows.

The vast majority of children said they experienced conflict with siblings and reported negative relationships at school. Difficulties are commonly attributed to 'being wound up' or 'annoyed' by others which in turn leads to 'moods', 'being angry or mad' and 'loosing my temper'. Teasing and name-calling are common features and friend-ships are affected.

> I had no friends at all. I had no one to play with. I was just walking around all day doing nothing. No one wants you... it's not a nice feeling at all.

A few children attempted to communicate a sense of what life is like having ADHD:

> It's like a computer without a hard drive it won't work will it!

> It's in your head. You can think up a brilliant idea but you just can't write it down and sometimes I think up ideas on the carpet but I just can't be bothered to lift my hand up.

The vast majority of conversations centred on how school staff res-ponded to problematic behaviour. Some approaches were viewed as helpful whereas others were seen as being less constructive or sensi-tive to the child's difficulties:

> I've had a few problems... the teacher used to call names to me. That's before I took the tablets. She used to say nasty things about me and my Mum told (the teacher). She's had a word with her but I was hoping she would have got the sack.

> It's better to have a teacher that doesn't shout at you, only shout at you when you've done something wrong.

Over three-quarters of the sample emphatically expressed a dislike of teachers shouting. Being more patient, understanding, less boring and 'get more work from us' were some ideas as to what teachers should do. Conversations with school staff about ADHD were rarely men-tioned. In one exceptional case the child found consolation through the teacher's interest:

> She (teacher) had to look it up in books and that. She knew every-thing about me. It helped me. They used to get people to sit by me a lot, help me work and that.

The majority of children did not mention specific details about the diagnosis and visits to the hospital or clinic seemed to blur into each other. Often other professionals had been previously involved with the family and some of the children were already visiting the paediatrician for other medical conditions. This may account for the vagueness and confusion surrounding diagnostic procedures. Diagnosis inevitably led to medication. It is this that makes many children feel that they are impaired in some way:

> It's a disease it just comes up. Mum didn't know I had it until I went to that doctor.

When the children were shown a photograph of a child who had just been told he had ADHD some indicated that the child might feel 'scared', 'confused', 'not know what's going on' and 'different'.

The main reason for the follow-up visits was seen as being for the doctor to ask questions about behaviour or 'how I've been', to find out whether the tablets were working. This was invariably linked, in their minds, with an increase in dosage if behaviour was not thought to have improved:

> I got to see him if I need to put my tablets up and that ... they just talk to you, if you've been good at school. If I've misbehaved. Things like that, boring.

What if your behaviour got worse?

> Then he'll (doctor) put my tablets up.

The majority of children thought the doctors were 'nice', 'good' and 'kind'. Some said they were asked questions although most were either not interested, ' I go and play with the toys', found it difficult to remember what had been said or viewed the main dialogue being between their parents and the doctor.

> He (doctor) asks my mum. She tells him everything but I ignore 'em.

Occasionally a child would hint at the powerful alliance and possible collusion between the doctor and their parent.

> My mum tells (doctor) what I've been up to and things like that and I deny it even if it is true. I don't like her telling on me. She's grassing me up. She never tells him good things. She always tells him bad things. I don't like it.

Reactions to subsequent medication

Most children spontaneously revealed that they were taking tablets (pills) before being shown the empty Ritalin packaging. On the face of it many students took a neutral stance and did not report either strong dislike or support for taking psychostimulants. However, the most frequently cited response to the question, 'what would it be like not having ADHD?' was 'I wouldn't have to take the tablets' which was often followed by 'hooray', 'that would be good that', 'brilliant really'.

> I'd be a lot happier. I wouldn't have to go out of my lessons to take tablets earlier. That would make me feel more better.

The most frequently reported view about psychostimulants was that that tablet had the power to alter 'naughty', 'bad', 'angry', 'moody' and 'noisy' behaviour, make them feel 'more calm' and increase concentration. However, the idea that the tablet could significantly alter behaviour was rarely backed up with evidence by relating specific school or home events. Since taking medication the majority of children still perceive themselves as having problematic behaviour.

Children commonly used language such as 'I need' and ideas such as 'I might faint or die' when asked what might happen if more than one tablet was forgotten. This shows a relationship of dependency. Sometimes children gave contradictory views about what they thought might or should happen and what actually did happen.

> I'd be naughty. Once I forgot to take one morning... and I came straight to school and forgot to take one at dinnertime.

And what happened?

> Now't

So does it matter if you forget to take one?

> It does matter because I'm being very naughty all the time.

Most children did not know how their tablets 'worked', 'they just control me that's all'. Some had vague biological notions such as they dissolve in the blood or stomach. The children who believed something is missing from their brain tended to see their tablets as replacing what is missing. Several children reported that it was taking medication which singled them out from other children and sometimes caused problems.

> I didn't want to take them. It was a good thing to stop me but in a way I just didn't want to be different. I wanted to be like everyone else.

> I don't take them. People make fun of me so that's when I don't take them.

A few children reported side effects they have directly experienced and several more hinted at the possibility of adverse side effects such as tiredness and loss of appetite. Most children seemed to be unperturbed by possible side effects.

A large proportion of children made a strong connection between dosage and how adults viewed the severity of their bad behaviour, although *bad* carried different meanings for different children.

> Like if I do more than six bad things I deserve more than one of my pills.

Many children indicated that they thought they would not be taking the tablets in adulthood, due to some natural maturing process which included being more able to control their behaviour. A few thought otherwise: 'I'll be taking them for the rest of my life probably.'

The impact of medication on behaviour and learning in school

In a parental survey more than half of the parents felt that medication had a huge positive effect on their child: the remainder felt it had some positive effect. Many parents, although emphasising behavioural change, felt that their children were achieving better at school. A few parents commented that improved behaviour at school and home did not always coincide.

In comparison the children rarely made dramatic claims, using word such as 'just a bit', 'not as much' or 'sometimes'

> They don't calm my nerves down enough cos when I take them I'm still naughty.

The effect of medication was mainly perceived in terms of behaviour but the children also reported improvements in academic achievement, 'having more friends', 'concentrating more', 'relaxed' and 'having a life now'.

Many children saw ADHD as a biological condition and did not associate it with the social barriers to participating fully in school life. However, some children identified school-based factors that could exacerbate or remediate their difficulties.

Did all your problems go away?

> Well some of them... when I was about eight and I had a better teacher, a way better teacher. She used to help me and everything and I had a good school report then.

Whilst some children noted change on the self-rating scales, it was clear that many perceived themselves as still having social needs and continued to experience social exclusion. Generally, the responsibility to conform was clearly seen to be the responsibility of the individual. These children thus acquiesce in their segregation from other pupils, possibly for pragmatic reasons.

Implications for practice
Informing children

Issues which arise when telling children that they have ADHD are: What do we tell them? Who tells them? And how? It is not an easy task as ADHD is still a vaguely defined problem which invokes various forms of discourse: academic, popular and advocacy. Some children are developing an informal knowledge based on overheard conversations. They may also be exposed to 'folklore inherent in perceptions of ADHD' which is directly related to professional practice (Maras *et al,* 1997). It would be better to open up more formal channels of communication.

It may be tempting to simplify these communications. However, Armstrong (1995) notes that attempts at child-friendly information have led to descriptions using metaphors of planes, radios and televisions: this implies that human beings are merely machines which need simple mechanical adjustment to be corrected.

This study suggests that information filtered through to children is too complicated, lacks practical ideas and disproportionately favours a medical orientation. There is a need for more balanced reporting and information, which emphasises the interaction of biological, social and psychological factors (Tannock, 1998). Even in an attractive and child-friendly explanatory booklet (Celltech, 2001), there is a failure to acknowledge environmental and interactionist factors which influence the child's behaviour. This places the onus of change solely on the child and presents medication as the only support available. Some children in our study may benefit from knowing that what is negative and unacceptable behaviour in one setting may be valuable and desirable in another. They can then begin to reframe certain behaviours as positive assets.

Medication as a control mechanism

Most of these children live their lives believing that ADHD is a real condition which they endure. This reality is reinforced through daily medication regimes which are closely associated, and sometimes confused, with the condition.

A common theme connecting many children's attitudes towards medication is that its purpose is to control, although the belief and real life events do not always match. One reason could be that the children are applying different criteria in terms of what constitutes better behaviour.

In studying the behaviour of the hyperactive child Weithorn (1979) made two important distinctions: that the child has difficulty coping and that the child is difficult to cope with. The children in this study emphasised the latter and many felt they were given tablets directly in relation to the problems they caused for others. This is relevant when evidence suggests that dosages effective for improving attention, control and learning are generally lower that those required to reduce inappropriate behaviour (Rapport and Kelly, 1991). It raises important questions about whose interests are best served by the prescribed levels of medication. If children themselves feel that there is little benefit from taking tablets, should parents insist on it and so expose children already under stress to the social disadvantages of drug taking?

The children in this study could not define a successful drug treatment. If they are to be engaged in the process of their own treatment should have a clearer understanding of what the treatment aims to achieve, in terms accessible to them.

Dealing with stigma

Many of the participants in the study saw having an ADHD diagnosis as a stigma. They had internalised messages that people think they are mad or bad. They have nothing to lose from forcefully expressing their feelings of despair and isolation. When this happens the responses of their classmates and family members confirm their worst fears about themselves. Newton *et al* (1996) suggest that this process of circular causation can be addressed through specific educational tools which foster the social psychology of acceptance and takes on the peer education role advocated by Hayward and Bright (1997). They recommend that stigma should be openly acknowledged and specific interventions applied to limit its effect.

Using sustained release methylphenidate is a possible means of reducing stigma and counteracting the social disadvantage associated with taking drugs in school. This appears to be an increasingly common practice, although information about it is limited. The lack of controlled comparison studies indicates that adults do not prioritise this as much as some of the children in this study do.

Sense of control and power

The overwhelming impression gained from the responses of the children is that they see themselves as passive recipients in a process over which they have little control. The external control is with the adults who define the problem and decide on the medication, usually with only a vaguely defined desirable outcome. The second external control is the medication itself, the tablets that either work or don't work. Even the potential power to decide whether to submit to medication is not a real one, as most children are given little choice in this matter.

It is of great concern that there now appears a generation of children in school who internalise descriptions of behaviours by believing themselves to be bad and who look to the power of tablets to control this internal deficiency. These perceptions have been shaped by their experiences with the adults around them but lack an awareness of the complexity of social behaviour. It also reduces opportunities to give children quality feedback and the practice of skills they need to manage their behaviour.

The work of White and Epston (1990) may provide some hope. Narrative therapy has proved useful in helping the young person to externalise the problem: a sense of control over a diagnosis rather than the other way round. Exploring what the problem does for other people enables them to develop in both a positive and negative sense and could help to identify to what extent the concept of ADHD is essentially an adult position, not shared by the child.

A pragmatic and helpful alternative to the medical perspective is the functional perspective. A functional assessment explores the combination of individual skills and environmental factors with regards to behaviour. In the school context disrupted interactions and the emotional effects seem to be of particular importance. These require broader based, creative interventions which incorporate the active involvement of all children, as well as the teachers and parents who deal with the day to day consequences. In the current educational climate it is tempting to defer to a medical model and never question the effect of educational policies or structures on the pupils' experience. This should not alienate or disempower teachers so that they are less likely to use complementary approaches. Rather than arguing for teachers to 'incorporate a medical perspective into their existing framework' (O'Regan, 2002), their expertise as educators and an understanding of the school environment and of children's different learning styles means they are well placed to be in the centre rather than on the margins of the professionals supporting these students. The challenge for schools and support services is to consider behaviour management not in terms of control and compliance but in terms of democracy, relevant curricula and flexibility. This will provide space for both pupils and teachers to identify and respond to the restraints within which they are operating. Teachers should then be able to make a genuine difference to these children's lives (Barton, 1999).

Conclusions

The number of children in this country who are currently receiving medication for ADHD is continuing to rise and we need to make sure that their views and needs are taken into account. There may well be a reluctance to do this with children who struggle to deal with negative situations they have been seen to create but it is important for such children to speak on their own behalf.

The children's stories we have been privileged to hear tell us there is a need for better, child-friendly information about ADHD. In order to avoid stigma, we must describe behaviours from within a functional model, rather than a medical model, and find alternative ways of providing social learning opportunities within school.

In defining pupils according to a powerful medical discourse, support services and educators may reduce opportunities to harness a child's individuality, complexity and creativity, particularly when trying to address their long term social needs. Professional collaboration across disciplines is essential as it is important that young people with ADHD do not lose out, caught between proponents and sceptics. Support services need to acknowledge the impact of debates around ADHD on children and young people and not leave them alone to deal with these struggles.

Genuine dialogue with children takes time. Some support services, particularly those operating within a behaviourist framework, have perhaps found it more convenient to plan responses to problems without the full participation of the young people themselves. As a consequence, success tends to be measured by reducing undesirable behaviours rather than gaining an understanding of how the child feels about themselves and their personal attributes. Debates about the effectiveness of provision and intervention need to include student views. Children with ADHD often find themselves in a *Catch 22* situation as lying is often cited as part of their condition. However, support services and educators need to believe that identifying the true situation is more important than an exploration of meanings and co-operative problem solving. This process involves an acceptance of diversity and difference.

To help them to express their views children and young people need structure, support, encouragement and above all genuine opportunities to recall experiences from which their perceptions are drawn. Professionals must develop and create opportunities to listen to the voices of the children they work with as their opinions can motivate adults into thinking more creatively about how the children's unmet needs can be addressed.

9

Turning up the volume: Pupils' voices on school improvement

Lynn Turner

Introduction

Existing at the margins

This chapter attempts to reflect the views of a group of pupils who are close to or at the margins.

- In a thriving city these pupils lived in one of the least privileged areas and are marginalised by dint of geography and socio-economic status

- The school itself lies at the margins being deemed as 'causing concern' and in danger of sliding down the Ofsted slope into 'serious weaknesses'

- Some, but not all, of the pupils consulted were at the margins within the school, at risk of exclusion and running foul of the internal discipline procedures

- In the literature on school improvement there is little representation of pupil perspective. However, I would argue that the pupils consulted here showed amazing insight into school improvement and school effectiveness issues even though they themselves would never have used these terms

Working with a school at the margins

The work described here was one piece amongst several which had been undertaken in this school around the area of behaviour, with the ultimate goal of school improvement. School improvement has been described in the literature as '...A sustained upward trend in effectiveness' (Reynolds *et al*, 2001, p2).

School effectiveness studies have identified factors associated with effective schools. According to Sammons *et al*, (1995) there are eleven factors for effective schools, including a learning environment which offers an orderly atmosphere and an attractive working environment, purposeful teaching including clarity of purpose and structured lessons, positive reinforcement which encompasses clear and fair discipline and feedback. Pupils' rights and responsibilities are also identified as a key factor and raising self-esteem, giving positions of responsibility and pupil control of work are included in this category.

The school is an 11-18 high school in what might be described as a socio-economically deprived area of a large city in the North of England. There are almost 600 pupils on role with about 50% entitled to free school meals. During the academic year 2000-2001 much work had been started by a new senior management team under an acting Head Teacher, the team showing much vision and enormous energy in turning around a school which had been causing concern. At a more recent Ofsted visit the school emerged quite well, but still with a low rating for pupil behaviour.

During the time that the Educational Psychology Service (EPS) have worked with the school the team had met with different staff groupings, carrying out interviews and leading discussion sessions, and had also interviewed some challenging pupils. The pupils' views were seen as important to making further improvements. The school had recently set up a school council so that the views of pupils could be heard. The work described here was a further attempt to elicit the views of pupils in the school on improving behaviour.

Pupil perspectives

Ruddock *et al* (1996) point to the general lack of pupil perspectives on school improvement and urge that pupil accounts of experiences should be heard and taken seriously in debates about learning in secondary schools. It might then follow that these voices should also be heard about issues relating to behaviour which so impact upon the opportunity to learn.

They also point out the fact that power relationships between teachers and pupils create difficulties in entering into a dialogue with young people about learning and behaviour. They suggest that many 'failing' schools would have been turned around if an agenda had been taken from pupils and used as a 'basis for planned change', and go on to argue that young people are observant and often capable of analytic and constructive comment, even though sometimes dismissed as 'not competent to judge these matters'. Further, they point to the 'bracketing out' of pupil voice and the exclusion of young people from the consultative process. Young people face complex relationships and situations outside school but are offered less responsibility and autonomy inside school.

Clough (1998) discusses the issues of 'voice', voice as a function of power or powerlessness and voice as a medium of narrative expression. He suggests that the task for research can be one of 'turning up the volume' on the depressed or inaudible voice. He also raises a more political and complex notion of voice around the question of who is listening to whom and why and in whose interests? Voice, according to Barton (1998), implies participating in decision making which will have a real impact upon lives.

Issues around listening to voice are problematic and the researcher must question his or her own stance, motives and constructs. 'The research act of listening to voice must always involve the (broadly defined) processes of both mediation and translation'. (Clough, *op cit*, p129)

In this chapter, although I'm trying to represent the voice of the pupil, I nevertheless have the final control over how that voice is ultimately represented. In so doing I have demonstrated the power of the adult professional over the pupil. To recognise this is only a small step in redressing the power imbalance which exists in society between adults and children, between professionals and non-professionals, between those who have a legitimate voice and those who do not.

Perhaps a more radical step would be supporting pupils to be researchers in their own right and giving them editorial control over what ultimately finds its way onto the page (see Pomerantz in chapter 11).

Consulting with children has become a much written and talked about issue over the past couple of decades, perhaps since the UN Convention of the Rights of the Child in 1989, the same year that the Children Act came into force in the UK. We are further urged to seek the views of children by the SEN Code of Practice (DfE, 1994) and its revision (DfES, 2002). This states that the views of children with special educational needs should be sought and taken into account.

The new Ofsted framework (2003) considers how well the school 'seeks, values and acts on pupils' views' and schools will be asked to provide evidence of this process. Surveys will be undertaken to see whether pupils believe that the school seeks their views and acts upon them, whether there are areas of school life they are not allowed to comment upon, whether they feel that their ideas are taken seriously and whether a school council exists in their school and if so, how that is perceived. This is a positive move because it puts consulting with children squarely on the agenda of school improvement.

The work of Ruddock *et al* (1996) outlines some principles which make a significant difference to learning. They encompass such ideas as:

- Respect for pupils as individuals
- Fairness to all pupils
- Autonomy
- Intellectual challenge
- Social support
- Security

These are set inside a framework of organisational structures, relationships with teachers and the quality of teaching. These principles resonate strongly with the findings in this chapter and the views expressed so passionately by the groups.

How the study was carried out

The approach to this study was inspired by an emancipatory research model. This emerged in part from debates around the area of disability studies and is alluded to in Corbett, 1998, as 'The facilitating of the politics of the possible by confronting social oppression at whatever level it occurs' (p 58).

The group of pupils consulted in this study were not disabled *per se*, but faced many disabling circumstances in their environment and their communities and were therefore at risk of social exclusion, and lacked any political voice.

It was decided that we, the researchers would ask the pupils, what were the questions we should be asking them about behaviour? To this end a team of three educational psychologists went to talk to the focus groups with an open agenda and no fixed idea of what the questions would be. We did not prompt the pupils but simply explored questions with them.

A focus group can be defined as 'A research technique that collects data through group interaction on a topic determined by the researcher' (Morgan, 1997, p 6).

Running the groups

The intention of illuminating the priorities of these groups and eliciting their own language, whilst unbounded by our own professional, adult constructs about either behaviour or school improvement, was a key element.

Participants were all from the same year group, year eight, with a gender mix, although predominantly girls, and a mix of more conforming pupils with those who ran foul of the school's behaviour systems. Group one had in it five girls and two boys and group two comprised three boys and six girls.

The original task was presented in two parts:

- We asked them to imagine that they were reporters on the local evening paper doing a piece on behaviour and how to improve it at their school. We asked them to describe what questions they would wish to ask

- Secondly, after some discussion, we introduced the idea of a rating scale, where 10 expressed the perfect school and 0 a school in chaos. We asked the pupils first of all to rate their school as it is now and then to describe what would need to happen to move from the given rating to the number one point up the scale

What the pupils say

The pupils expressed strong feelings about certain areas of school life, with key themes of bullying, teaching and learning, behaviour management or discipline, school facilities, school uniform and relationships between pupils and teachers. What linked these themes was the pupils' strong sense of fairness or injustice.

Views on bullying

We were surprised at just how perceptive these groups of children were around the issue of bullying. They recognised not only that pupils bully pupils but also that teachers bully pupils and that pupils bully teachers.

In bullying between pupils the question of 'grassing' (telling) was discussed. Should you tell or not? What would be the repercussions?

> People should just own up if they are getting bullied. I know it's grassing but you could get more hurt if you don't grass.

> If you tell on them they bully you worse anyway.

There was a feeling that teachers could sort out the problem in school but not outside of school, where revenge could still be wrought. One pupil also identified an age element, where older pupils pick on the younger ones.

On the issue of teachers as bullies:

> Teachers do bully kids. What about when you are being bullied by the teacher like Miss X... she used to bully everyone.

On the issue of kids bullying teachers:

> Because they (the kids) are bullying the teacher aren't they? She tells them what to do and they just carry on for her. She tries really hard and at the end she just cries.

The issue of fairness was raised in regard to the above kind of bullying and a concern about teacher feelings, and whether or not some teachers really wanted to be in the school because of how the pupils behave. The theme of fairness was raised many times throughout the groups' discussions but more often in relation to the pupils' own feelings. This taking on of the teachers' perspective and the degree of empathy expressed here was unique.

Views on teaching and learning
The general consensus here was that many teachers talk too much, that there is too much writing to do in class and not enough fun in learning. There was also an issue for some pupils about not understanding what the teachers were teaching them.

> Sometimes you can (make sense of what the teacher is saying) but sometimes you can't, most of the time you can't.

> They just carry on blabbing and you get bored.

> [Teachers] Going on, talking forever.

> In science we have never, ever done a practical, it has always been writing out of text books.

The themes of coherence and connectedness in learning emerge from the literature on school improvement and pupils' views in this area. Whilst the concept of intellectual challenge is a factor in effectiveness so too is clarity of purpose. The importance of lessons being varied so as to engage pupil interest cannot be overstated. Too often the active learning so apparent in many primary schools is sacrificed in the secondary phase and passive learning can predominate, leading to disengagement. There is also a fine line to be drawn between academic challenge and the need for appropriate differentiation. Pupils can become disengaged if work is either too challenging or not challenging enough.

Views on behaviour management
In the area of behaviour pupils had some views on classroom discipline. They felt that some pupils wanted to learn and others did not. A view was expressed that in year nine pupils should be set (grouped), dependent on their prior behaviour in year eight rather than on academic prowess, so that pupils who were good could learn

if they wanted to. They also expressed the view that teachers should be stricter and voiced some frustration about the slow start to lessons whilst the teacher waited for everyone to take their coats off.

> At the beginning of the lesson it's like twenty minutes waiting because everyone is getting their coat off... and then we get done even more for that.

Pupils also had something to say about rewards too. There was a general view that there should be more rewards, some small rewards like Mars Bars and some really big rewards like a TV. Going on trips and money were also mentioned as possible rewards. Food was considered to be a good motivator of positive behaviour:

> Why don't they have more rewards and more achievements 'cos kids would be so eager to get pop or Mars Bars wouldn't they?

> When you are sat in a lesson and you're really warm and so hungry you would work really hard to try to get a bottle of pop or a bag of crisps or something.

However, the overwhelming weight of discussion was on sanctions and a variety of views were expressed. One voice spoke for corporal punishment but this was an isolated view. There was much debate about the effectiveness of being on report as a deterrent, detentions and use of the exclusion room within school. There was comparatively little reference made to exclusion from school but when it was referred to it was seen as the school 'giving up on you'.

There were mixed views on detentions: some pupils felt they didn't make a difference, some thought there should be more of them. There was certainly a view that, where there were detentions, they should be longer and taken more seriously by teachers.

> I had a detention the other day and they just let me off with it.

> When you have got half hour detentions, after about ten minutes, they let you go because they haven't got time for you.

It was interesting to note that the pupils interpretation of being 'let off' was not seen as an act of benevolence on the part of the teacher but as the teacher not being committed to them, or giving up on them, rather as an exclusion from school was viewed.

The on-site exclusion room provoked much discussion too. Some pupils viewed it as quite an easy option, others thought it made pupils worse and some pupils preferred to be in there than in their lessons.

More pupils want to go in there, it's better than class.

Yeah (it's nice), it calms you down.

Pupils need an orderly atmosphere in which to learn and the effectiveness literature emphasises the importance of positive reinforcement and clear and fair discipline. Adults' perceptions of what is reinforcing to pupils may be very different from the views of the pupils themselves, and likewise with sanctions. In managing behaviour effectively it is clear that a good reciprocal dialogue is crucial.

Views on school facilities

The majority of concerns expressed were about the poor state of the building and issues about toilets. There were strongly held views about the school having installed Closed Circuit Television (CCTV) in the school toilets.

Pupils were generally aware of the poor state of some of the school building. Although there are some new blocks, they focused on the rotting windows that let in cold and rain and places where the floor was coming up in the older parts of the school. Pupils felt that these features had an impact on behaviour because if pupils were cold they would be reluctant to take off coats in school and this lead to them getting into trouble. Pupils also commented about positive changes like interactive white boards and would like to see more computers during normal lessons. They said that when displays were put up that they got torn down or spoiled by others.

Pupils were passionate about toilets and the issue of CCTV cameras. Whilst some pupils could see the point of having cameras for security because someone had previously started a fire in the toilets, others could not see the point. However, there was total consensus about the poor state of toilets, lack of toilet rolls, lack of hot water, poor cleanliness, smell, and doors without locks. The boys felt particularly strongly about the fact that their toilets were always open and the girls were locked because the girls had toilet roll! The girls felt it unfair that they had to 'walk round for ages' to get a key for the toilet. This comment sums up the view of the majority:

I think the toilets are that bad that no one hardly likes using them. You'd rather wee yourself than go to the toilet.

Views on uniform

Mixed views were expressed about the need for uniform and whether there was a link between uniform and behaviour. Some pupils felt that they had to wear school uniform to make the school look smart for visitors and inspectors.

> I think we should do [wear school uniform], even if we don't like it, to make our school look better.

The comment above was linked to another observation about a school in the south of the city where pupils had to wear blazers, the conclusion being that their own school wasn't strict enough!

On the other hand:

> We shouldn't have to wear school uniform because it has nothing to do with learning really.

Issues around jewellery and uniform were strongly linked to feelings of fairness and respect. However, there was a dilemma between wanting to assert their own individuality in what they wore and the knowledge their dress also says something about their school.

Views on relationships

There was a feeling, especially voiced in the first group, that some teachers did not want to be at their school. Others issues raised were around respect and fairness.

> I think some teachers don't want to be here because of how pupils behave.

> They [teachers] might think they're doing everything for us and we are just throwing it back in their face.

These comments link back to the bullying of teachers by pupils referred to earlier in the chapter. There was also a sense under sanctions of a perceived lack of commitment by some teachers when they did not see out a detention, or especially when pupils were excluded from school. When asked what they would ask teachers the response was simply:

> Why do they give up on us?

On respect:

> I think the teachers should be more polite towards us because they are awful to us...

> Teachers need to treat kids with respect and then we might treat them with respect as well.

The pupils felt passionately about fairness, and this was a theme that ran throughout all topics.

> Yeah, if you get sent out [of class] and they say, I need to hear both sides of the story, and they just hear the teachers' side.

> If someone's had a good reputation and they do something wrong no one believes you because they've been good all their lives haven't they? [They should] listen to both sides of the story. If someone has had a bad reputation before it doesn't mean to say that they actually were bad at this time.

Listening was a theme difficult to distinguish from fairness, the two very often going hand in hand. On a positive note, one pupil was part of the new school forum and commented:

> Yeah, I am in the school forum and they listen to us, like the dining room were boring and when we asked them to paint it, now they have done, there are loads of bright colours in there now.

Less positive were:

> Nobody listens to me.

And in response to the question, what makes you stressed?

> Not being listened to.

Relationships underpin the functioning of any organisation and the school is no exception to this. There are complex sets of relationships at work between senior management and staff, between departments, between teaching and non-teaching staff and so on. Layered on top of this are the relationships between staff and different pupils' groupings. In an emotionally literate organisation all of these groupings will feel valued and 'heard' by others within the organisation. What is often clear in any organisation is that there is a pecking order of which groups are most heard, and a sense that the natural order means that pupils are least heard. Adults need to be sensitive to the tone and manner of their discourse with pupils but also there need to be mechanisms in place for seeking pupils' views, listening to their concerns and acting upon them.

Implications of what the pupils had to say

The concerns of pupils at this high school regarding education and the learning environment may not be unique. Readers may have frequently encountered them. It is possible now to juxtapose these views with what we know from research about school effectiveness, where the voice of the pupil is usually totally absent. This is an attempt to turn up the volume and to ask ourselves: how can these pupils be given more of a say in their own education?

It is helpful here to draw upon the context of school effectiveness research and the eleven factors for effective schools outlined by Sammons *et al.* (1995). In particular, the issues around learning environment, purposeful teaching, positive reinforcement, and pupils' rights and responsibilities.

In addition Ruddock *et al* (1996) propose a framework which describes the relationship between organisational structures and relationships with teachers and the pupils themselves. Underpinning the structures and relationships are the principles of:

- Respect
- Fairness
- Autonomy
- Challenge
- Security
- Support

What the pupils need in order to be effective are:

- Sense of self as a learner
- Status in school
- Overall purpose in learning
- Control over their own lives
- Sense of future

One of the first issues raised by pupils was bullying and the debate about whether it was okay, or even safe, to tell. This relates to one of the fundamental principals of security, which is essential to self-esteem and allaying feelings of anxiety. A further issue was raised in this section about fairness in relation to teachers and pupils. These pupils felt strongly the unfairness to teachers when bullied by pupils and vice versa. Although the conditions of learning framework specifies fairness to all pupils, the pupils interviewed in our study seemed to have a unique perspective and degree of empathy around the issue of fairness to teachers.

One of the factors for effective schools is identified as purposeful teaching. Within this broader area it is particularly around clarity of purpose where these pupils seemed to find difficulty. They were not always clear about information conveyed to them in subject areas. In terms of the conditions of learning this impacts upon their sense of self as a learner and their overall purpose in learning. In terms of the quality of teaching most lessons which have clear focus and content, a variety of pace and activity, and convey the important message that the teacher enjoys teaching that subject. Some of these pupils seemed not to understand the focus and content of some lessons, questioned the variety or balance of some lessons and questioned the teacher's enjoyment of teaching them. They could understand why some teachers did not enjoy teaching at their school, when pupils were bullying them. The importance of intellectual challenge is emphasised when pupils experience learning as a 'dynamic, engaging and empowering activity'. There was evidence that these pupils found some of their learning experiences quite the opposite, whilst finding the work challenging. This was conveyed as a sense of bafflement and confusion about its demands.

Pupils' notions of behaviour management were also underpinned by their relationships with teachers and the degree of commitment they saw in teachers. Sammons *et al* (*op cit*), stress the importance of clear and fair discipline and Ruddock *et al* (*op cit*), further emphasise the need to explain to pupils the reason for particular rules. It has long been recognised as good practice in the area of positive behaviour management that pupils have a part to play, along with parents, in developing behaviour policy and the ways it is put into practice. Verbal feedback is arguably the most important tool that teachers have to manage behaviour but this must be done in the context of respect, fairness, security and support. One of the key factors in becoming an effective school and therefore an improving school is that the learning environment provides an orderly atmosphere. This is only achievable when other factors which underpin positive behaviour management are in place.

The pupils in this study also identify the environment features they find uncomfortable, unpleasant or demeaning. An effective school has a positive learning environment which is attractive as well as orderly.

Our pupils expressed strong feelings about school uniform, allied to perceptions about their opinions not being valued and adults not keeping their word. There was a view that although consultation had taken place, it had not been acted upon and was therefore tokenistic. The 'conditions of learning' model draws the relationship between organisational matters about rules and regimes and how this impacts upon the pupils' sense of status within the school, their sense of control over their own lives and also the principle of autonomy. Pupils' rights and responsibilities are key factors in an effective school.

Conclusions

In an educational era where we are encouraged to seek the views of children and take them into account, there is remarkably little evidence of the voice of the pupil in any literature relating to school effectiveness or school improvement.

The views expressed by these pupils described, in this chapter, were heartfelt and at times passionate. It is hard to convey the animation and intense feeling present in the room during the focus group interviews. Without doubt pupils have opinions which can be validated by research and unique perspectives on what goes on in school.

What was conveyed with great strength was the pupils' sense of fairness and their ability to empathise with teachers who were suffering the effects of challenging behaviour and bullying (*sic*). They were able to understand in a remarkably mature way why some teachers did not wish to teach them. Their account was also quite striking in their perception that some teachers lacked commitment to them, and that a greater 'strictness' was viewed by pupils as a greater sense of commitment, if carried out with fairness and respect. Exclusions were certainly seen as the school 'giving up on you'.

Listening was also a spontaneous theme for these groups of pupils. It is clear that listening itself is not enough and that to have a sense of actually being heard, the listening needs to be validated by action on the part of all of us who work in education; the school and the services which support schools in improving, but most importantly those in high office who have the power to give legitimacy to pupils' voices through our systems and structures.

It is encouraging that there is now widespread recognition, even in such conservative institutions as Ofsted, of the need to listen to children and it is a legitimate role of support services to help schools to do this effectively. In the past, educational psychologists have been accused of propping up systems which repress the pupil voice, for example, by using assessment tools which contributed to the over-representation of black pupils in special schools and in consulting pupils in a tokenistic way as part of statutory processes. Educational Psychology Services in the twenty first century should see action research as a responsibility which enables them to:

- facilitate the pupil voice
- support schools in acting on the findings of research
- take an active part in school improvement

Services must set aside time for these crucial activities in order to become true agents of change, taking on the dual activities of support and challenge through evidence based-practice.

10
Children and the curriculum

Richard Gamman

Introduction

In this chapter I contend that the way in which the National Curriculum is structured says much about how society conceptualises children as subjects, to be given what they need by adults who know best. As a consequence children understand their educational experience in terms of the dominant narratives of attainment levels and preparation for employment. I argue that helping children to understand the values that underlie subject study is essential to their growth into engaged and participatory members of society.

Education, like politics, economics, clothing, music and many other facets of society, is subject to cyclical change. In the political domain the socialist movement currently lacks the vibrancy it possessed during much of the twentieth century and within education, as part of the same social trend, the concept of a child-centred curriculum remains unfashionable. Yet, it is a remarkably short time since a government education ministry issued guidance to schools suggesting that 'best practice in English' might be identified by classrooms in which '...pupils are seen:

> Working on tasks which they have chosen and which they direct for themselves; Reading literature for enjoyment, responding to it critically and using that reading for learning (DES, 1989, para. 3.4)

Priorities in educational policy making have shifted enormously since this report was published and a curriculum which is tightly and centrally determined and teacher-led at the classroom level is the current orthodoxy.

This chapter takes the subject area of English as a case study, although the conclusions drawn may be applied more widely. I began by talking to groups of eleven and twelve year old children about their experiences of English during their final year of primary school and first year of secondary school. It soon became clear that the children were certainly not working on tasks they have chosen or direct themselves. So what messages do children derive about the meaning of the subjects they study, what is their motivation to learn and how does school life impact on their development into adult citizens?

Pomerantz's argument that involving able underachievers in their curriculum enhances motivation is echoed here. Inadequate engagement and consequently a sterile educational experience is the norm rather than a problem affecting specific subgroups. Teachers are seen as marginalised figures within education, often working to an agenda which is not theirs, driven by values they do not share. The chapter concludes with a discussion of how the participation of pupils can be increased. Such an objective may currently feel like trying to hold back the tide; I prefer to think of being ready for when the tide turns and flows once more towards increased autonomy for individual teachers and pupils.

Values and the National Curriculum

The National Curriculum and subsequent developments of it such as the National Literacy Strategy (DfEE, 1998) have been regarded by successive governments as key tools in promoting pupil attainment and maintaining progress throughout their education. The National Curriculum, it is argued, ensures that children receive a common educational entitlement across the maintained sector, ensuring that pupils who change schools in our increasingly mobile society can do so with a minimum of disruption. Governments now regard the school curriculum as the key tool at their disposal in the drive to 'raise standards', although there is considerable evidence that school improvement is concerned with a much wider range of factors than the curriculum alone. For example, a shared vision and goals and effective home-school partnerships have been shown to be important characteristics of effective schools (Sammons, Hillman and Mortimer, 1995). However, what the curriculum provides is the data on which performance may be judged and institutions compared.

Our society is obsessed with performance data and our government wedded to the idea that an improvement in public services may be achieved by comparing outcome data of different service providers. So, we see league tables of schools and hospitals, effectiveness rankings of social services departments and Local Education Authorities (LEA's). Service providers have become increasingly adept at focusing their efforts on the targets that are to be measured and schools are no exception to this. The important data for primary schools are the SATs exams taken by pupils at the end of their final year. Similarly, at secondary level the Year 9 SATs provide some data but are relatively less important than the public exams at GCSE, AS and A level.

At the end of the primary phase of education the entitlement to a broad and challenging National Curriculum which was envisaged at its inception has been lost in a narrow focus on the three core subjects which are examined (English, Maths and Science). Furthermore, the importance to schools of the results of the data from these examinations means that there is enormous pressure to teach to the test, resulting in an increase in 'transmission teaching' which emphasises the development of competencies rather than conceptual development (Askew *et al*, 1997).

Surveys of English teachers have consistently found that they believe that their subject needs to focus primarily on the development of personal growth in their pupils. This model of the subject emphasises the relationship between language and learning in the individual and the way in which literature impacts upon children's lives (Goodwyn and Findlay, 1999). Historically, English teachers have valued the opportunity to construct courses which are meaningful and relevant to the local circumstances of the children they teach (Stevens, 1998). However, the National Literacy Strategy (NLS), regarded by the government as a major success and agent for improving literacy standards in schools, is a technical approach to delivering a body of skills. The philosophy of English teaching which underlies the NLS is in dramatic contrast to the social and democratic values English teachers see as being at the core of their subject.

The implication of this research is that teachers in the subject area of English are teaching to a curriculum whose values they don't share. This is a dangerous situation as the values which underlie the curriculum define children's understanding of its purpose. Currently, English teachers do not play the central role in planning the curriculum they teach and they have little commitment to the ethos which underlies it. Consequently, they tend not to communicate to children their views of why it is important for them to study the subject they teach. If the purpose of the curriculum is not communicated to children in explicit terms, they must infer it. This process leads to disengagement and marginalisation of children who discern values they do not share. The following section explores the ability of some children to describe the reasons they study English at school.

Children's understanding of the values which underlie subject study

Children talking about their literacy experiences describe the pleasure they derive from reading fiction and the excitement of creative writing. These descriptions are of activities linked strongly to the personal growth model of English to which teachers were predominantly committed. However, they were in contrast to children's understanding of the purpose of learning to read and write. In a study involving over 100 participants aged between ten and twelve there was just one reference to learning to read and write as a leisure skill. Far more commonly children spoke of the acquisition of skills for employment and to achieve academic success, defined in terms of examination grades (Gamman, 2002).

The objective of acquiring literacy skills for adulthood is the dominant justification for the current English curriculum. In his foreword to the NLS primary 'framework for teaching' (DfEE, 1998), David Blunkett, then Secretary of State for Education, wrote as his first sentence 'All our children deserve to leave school equipped to enter a fulfilling adult life.'

The implications of regarding education, particularly at the primary phase, as simply about preparation for adulthood are unacceptable. A child's time at school is an important part of his or her present life and so needs to possess intrinsic and immediate value, not merely be seen as a means to an end. The acquisition of literacy at this age is about – and I select from a very long list – fantasy, the discovery of new knowledge and the exploration of feelings and relationships. It is important for children to have sufficient grasp of this so that they can understand the purpose of learning to read and write in a wider context.

Similarly, the other main reason for acquiring literacy given by the children, to achieve academic success, is very limiting. This is particularly so if pupils regard teachers as being interested in their individual success only in terms of whole school performance, 'They wanted us to do good in SATs so that it would make the school look good' (a secondary aged girl reflecting on Year 6 SATs) (Gamman, 2002, p 90).

This perception represents a very profound indictment of the way in which outcome data are driving educational processes, with children not only being regarded by teachers as a means to institutional ends, but recognising this reality themselves. In this sense the interests of all children are being marginalised as their personal development needs are sacrificed to the needs of the school, LEA or to a government which has become hostage to arbitrary measures of attainment.

A couple of examples will illustrate that the above argument is not simply derived from a selected quote of one child. In a recent discussion with an Inspector working for a Local Education Authority I foolishly suggested that her role meant that she was concerned with the bigger picture and was rarely aware of the educational experience of individual children. This was firmly denied with the explanation that she was in a position to give me with the names of 30 targeted 10 year olds, who, if they could achieve level 4 instead of their projected level 3, would ensure that her LEA would meet the performance target agreed with the Department for Education and Skills. This was an arbitrary target, agreed at a theoretical level between a senior education officer in an LEA and a civil servant in London. This meeting was necessitated by a political promise made some years earlier by a politician who is now in a different post. It means that a cohort of children attaining in the low average range are being targeted for extra support. These are not the most needy children, but those who happen to be close to this inherently meaningless threshold and who have assumed strategic importance because of the data-driven, product-led emphasis in our current education system.

This cannot be regarded as an isolated example of misguided practice in the context of programmes of study produced by the DfES specifically aimed at children who have achieved level 3 in their year 6 SATs and need to catch up either during the summer holidays before joining secondary school or through 'booster classes' when they are there. Notably, children who have achieved below a level 3 have not been eligible for this support. This is not an argument against striving for high academic standards; it is an attempt to point out the absurdity of focusing resources on a group of children who are distinguished only by their proximity to an arbitrary attainment score.

It is clear that the values which underlie the curriculum are primarily concerned with institutional objectives rather than with the personal development of each child. The following section considers what this reveals about the social construction of children within the education system.

The conceptualisation of children in the education system

Children may be conceptualised within society and particularly in relation to adults in a number of different ways. Lloyd-Smith and Tarr (2000) consider four different models of childhood which are helpful in exploring current educational structures:

1. Children as possessions: The child within this model has no rights independent of the adult until majority and his or her needs are subservient to the needs of the adult

2. Children as subjects: This model is characterised by the idea that children need adult protection but that in all respects the adult determines what the needs of the child are. Implicit is the concept that adults know best at all times

3. Children as participants: The central concept of this model is that children have the right to be consulted about any decisions that will have an impact upon them

4. Children as citizens: Within this conceptualisation of childhood children possess the right to make choices and take actions independently of adults.

The phrase, 'children as possessions' might be regarded as one which allows us to relax in the thought that 'at least we've moved on from there'. However, closer examination of the way in which our focus on product data impacts on children should make us less comfortable. When a child who achieves in the low average attainment range is selected for booster tuition, whilst another child who is lower attaining is not eligible, it seems disingenuous to argue that this is for the child's own good. The outcome may or may not be beneficial for the child but the real agenda here is that of the adults and the child is a tool, a means to a statistical end.

With the exception of the situations discussed above, the dominant model of the National Curriculum is of children as subjects, to whom the curriculum is delivered. Implicit in the expectation that almost all children will move through the education system at a rate of one step a year is the notion of a normal child following a predetermined path towards maturity. The concept of entitlement is strongly emphasised in the documentation which supports the National Curriculum (Oliver, 2001). The content of that is largely determined by adults outside individual schools and there is no right of refusal, so teachers are also in some senses subjects.

The idea of children as participants in the decision-making about their educational programmes is far from the current orthodoxy in schools. This is despite the fact that the UK is a signatory to the UN Convention on the Rights of the Child 1989, which states that children have a right to express their views on all matters of concern to them. For most children their views in relation to the curriculum will first be requested about the limited subject choices they can make at Key Stage 4. Prior to this, children are increasingly encouraged to state their own targets in relation to the curriculum. However, this can be viewed in terms of the exertion of power within the social institution as adults coerce children to subscribe to a particular set of values.

Interestingly, the impact of other disciplines, such as social work, where there is a much stronger emphasis on eliciting children's views, is exerting some influence on practices within education. The expectation that children will be consulted about the provision they are receiving is made explicit in the area of children with Special Educational Needs (DfES, 2001). It may be argued that, almost by definition, the *one-size-fits-all* expectation of the National Curriculum has already failed to meet the needs of these children so that asking them for their views is not so threatening to the status quo as inviting the contributions of all children.

There is a limited history of children within the UK being involved in schools as citizens. The movement for schools to have pupil councils has been a significant factor in introducing children to the concept of representation. However, such councils are beyond the scope of this chapter because they do not typically address themselves to matters of curriculum content so much as social organisation. It is, however, interesting that the government appears to recognise that something is awry in the progression of children from their position as subjects within the education system to active citizens in adulthood. This is apparent in a failure of young people to vote and a relative lack of student political activism despite a huge increase in higher education numbers. Rather than examine from first principles the models of childhood that children experience in school, the government has chosen instead to introduce Citizenship Education into the curriculum. The content of this curriculum and its likely impact on children will be considered in a later section.

The impact of being a *subject*

The dominant model of childhood in our schools is of children as subjects and the imposition of a centrally determined curriculum places teachers in a similarly powerless position. In secondary schools, in particular, where the government correctly insists that teachers possess a high level of subject specialism, the lack of control over curriculum content undermines professionalism. This effect is present even in the language currently used about teaching. The phrase 'delivering the curriculum' for example implies transmission rather than engagement. Most important of all, however, is the link between values and the curriculum. All subject areas are repositories of values; the growth of self-awareness in English, evaluation of evidence in History or precision of observation in Science (Butroyd, 2001).

Good teachers come to the classroom with a commitment to the value systems of their subject but delivering an externally imposed curriculum means that these are unlikely to shine through. A good teacher who has had a significant input into devising a curriculum will ensure that these values are made explicit as children learn. Certainly, they will have commitment to the responses they give to the question, 'Why do we have to learn this?' which has characterised generations of classroom dialogue. The consequence of a curriculum not based on the values of the teachers who deliver it is that a vacuum exists. Teachers do not make explicit the values of the subject and children must therefore determine for themselves the values which underlie what they are being taught and identify achieving exam success and training for adulthood as the most important value.

Under this system, therefore, children are recipients of a curriculum over which neither they nor their teachers have significant control and which allows for little adaptation to take account of local social or cultural variation. In this context the lack of participation in discussion about curriculum content or values will have the effect of generating in children a sense of powerlessness, low self-efficacy and ultimately a lack of commitment to the courses they are expected to study.

Children may then express a lack of engagement in a number of different ways. On the one hand, there are those children who are most readily recognisable as being at the margins; those who reject the education system and who, disaffected, either receive their education in special provision or receive no education at all. On the other, there are those who remain within the system, who may in another sense be legitimately regarded as marginalised. These children may regard their education in the terms of the current orthodoxy and focus on achieving exam success so that they can proceed on to higher education and employment. What they may lack, however, is the sense of autonomy that equips them to play an active part in society either at a political or community level.

Clearly, it is inappropriate to regard the growth of individualism and disengagement with political processes as exclusively a function of education and in particular the National Curriculum. Nevertheless, as the government regards education as a key tool in rectifying these perceived problems through the introduction of a Citizenship curriculum it is legitimate and appropriate to speculate on how the curriculum as it is currently conceived impacts on the development of the individual.

Citizenship education and children as 'participants'

Citizenship Education is now a statutory entitlement within schools and the structure of this element of the curriculum was largely shaped by a Qualifications and Curriculum Authority report that identified three main objectives:

> ...learning ... self-confidence and socially and morally responsible behaviour both in and beyond the classroom, both towards those in authority and towards each other

> ...learning about and becoming helpfully involved in the life and concerns of their communities...

> ...learning about and how to make themselves effective in public life (QCA, 1998: p 11-13)

Although there is a practical element to the recommendations in this report it is notable that it relates primarily to engagement in community projects outside the school. There is no re-evaluation of how children are conceptualised in school. Consequently the expectation appears to be that, with this addition to the curriculum, children will be enabled to make the transition from their status as passive recipients of a curriculum to active citizens, presumably at the point when they leave school.

The opportunity to participate in decision making about issues which concern children is not simply a right as contained in the 1989 UN Convention, it is an essential element in learning how to behave as an adult. The comparison of expecting a seventeen year old to learn to drive through classroom tuition alone is not far fetched. Of course, practical experience, under skilled guidance, is necessary to learn the skills of driving. Similarly, learning to be an active participant in society requires increasing autonomy and engagement in decision making throughout childhood and adolescence. The reality is that the only way children can comment on and shape the curriculum they receive in school is to reject it. Then support systems are called upon and an alternative curriculum is often provided. It is arguable that the model of citizenship which children are being taught through the reality of their daily experience in school is that rejection and refusal to engage with systems are the only way to effect change.

Ways to increase pupil participation in the curriculum

The following section explores a number of options for increasing pupil reflection on and involvement with the curriculum in schools. This is based on the premise that if children are to become active and engaged citizens they need to become used to participation, at least, in schools. Regarding children as subjects necessitates them accepting a submissive role in which they accept that others make judgements in their best interests. This is not a good preparation for involvement in an active democracy.

A starting point for this objective of increased participation is to make explicit to children the processes which are important, even within the current centrally determined curriculum. The model for this task is in the increased expectation that teachers will tell children the objectives of individual lessons, rather than simply expect them to infer them. These are typically skills-based 'product' objectives eg 'generate, cluster and organise ideas into a planned sequence of paragraphs' (National Literacy Strategy, Framework for Teaching English Years 7-9. DfEE, 1998, p 18). Such transparency in short term objectives should and can be transferred to the longer-term process objectives through an expectation that teachers will attempt to transmit to children the values that are inherent in curriculum subjects. This will equip children with an understanding of the purposes behind the subjects they study and enable them to talk about reasons for study in more expansive terms than 'to get a job' or 'to get a GCSE'. Debate about why we study, often framed by children as a challenge to teachers, is an excellent forum for promoting participation and reflection on the learning process. Furthermore, as Pomerantz reports from his study, many teachers find such opportunities for debate stimulating.

Discussion of process objectives such as 'critically analyse textual material for sources of bias' can only be fully understood through meaningful curriculum activities. For this reason it is important that sufficient local control is reintroduced into the curriculum that LEAs, schools and individual teachers can construct courses which are relevant to their local circumstances and cultural contexts. The National Curriculum needs to be a framework into which activities to which teachers enjoy to and children relate can be incorporated. The release of some control to a local level will result in an increased sense of empowerment and personal autonomy for teachers, characteristics associated with lower job stress and disaffection. Curriculum activities which link into local resources and priorities can allow the teaching of Citizenship to reside within the traditional curriculum subjects, where a full range of social democratic values may be taught. Geography is the appropriate context for consideration of issues of immigration and asylum; History for the impact of different political systems and the importance of an informed electorate; English for developing skills of self-expression and exploring the impact of oppression on the individual. Furthermore, the entire curriculum needs to be concerned with encouraging independence of thought and developing skills of reflection, enquiry and debate.

Increased emphasis needs to be given to the level of pupil choice within the curriculum. This need not be the unstructured choice which is ridiculed in critiques of child-centred approaches to education but opportunities to make genuine choices of equivalent activities. Children do not generally like highly restricted tasks such as writing the ending to an uncompleted story, tasks that restrict creativity and deny links to their own lives (Gamman, 2002). It will still be possible to incorporate the monitoring of pupil progress, setting of targets and elements of structured teaching, which are the current orthodoxy, within such proposals.

Little consideration was given to the views of children in schools during the planning of the National Curriculum or in subsequent alterations to it. There is clearly a case for ongoing research, sponsored by curriculum planners, into children's perceptions of the education they are receiving. The fact that this does not occur, except through the highly subjective means of the Ofsted inspections, indicates how thoroughly the model of children as subjects is established within our culture.

However, the prospects for greater pupil participation in the structure of their educational experience are not good. The government is thoroughly wedded to the concept of tight central control over the curriculum as this provides a tool for comparing institutions and shaming the lowest achieving; the preferred model for raising standards. This control necessitates the conceptualisation of children as subjects and recipients, largely disenfranchised along with their teachers in the construction of their learning experiences. At the same time there is a concern that young people are not participating in society, at least not through the established electoral system, and this is a concern to politicians. Currently, there is no indication that any linkage between these effects is acknowledged. Rather, the government seeks to address perceived problems through additional bolt on elements to the curriculum: most notably literacy and numeracy strategies and a Citizenship curriculum. Increasing the engagement of children requires the relinquishing by central government of some of the power taken over the years. This will require a considerable cultural shift. It will be necessary to use continued evidence-based argument to hasten this shift but, perhaps most importantly, to allow time for the cyclical nature of democratic processes to take effect.

11
Belper School Able Underachievers Group 2002-2003

Michael Pomerantz

Introduction and background

It is a privilege to share this ongoing story which began within an earlier project researching Able Underachievers. They are one group at risk of marginalisation within schools. The work began when I interviewed 26 Able Underachievers in Derbyshire and subsequently wrote a book entitled *Listening to Able Underachievers: Creating Opportunities for Change* (2002) with my wife Kathryn Pomerantz. The study focused upon the perspectives of the Able Underachievers themselves and addressed the twin questions of why pupils with ability might underachieve and what could be done to reduce under-achievement.

We wrote a first version of the book and asked colleagues and friends to give it a 'critical read' and tell us what they thought about it. While the reactions tended to be generally favourable and encouraging, one particular reader felt the work was unfinished. He suggested that we ought to write something quite different which was much more prac-tical and contained more suggestions specifically about boosting the attainments of Able Underachievers and focused on schools rather than in the wider community. This was quite an inviting proposal as we knew that there was a good deal of fascinating activity already taking place within schools, as had been reflected during the initial school visits where the interviews for the book took place. I have inspiring memories of teachers and pupils telling their own narratives of the success of specific events and activities which they had created. I was particularly pleased to hear stories which reflected both pride and optimism that something constructive and original was happening to raise the aspirations and output of Able Underachievers.

At one stage I thought the next step would simply be to interview more pupils and staff in order to continue to capture a stronger picture of all the positive steps that were being taken, especially since Ofsted had announced that it would be looking for specific evidence of what schools are doing with their more able pupils.

However, developments within the field of research on social inclusion suggest that professionals need to be more sensitive and politically aware in how they go about their work. The normal practice has been for academic researchers, who are always adults, to mount studies from their own vested interests which include serious pressure to get their studies published. This has usually been done without recourse to early and purposeful consultation with the pupils who are the subjects of the research. Normal research frequently involves adults asking questions of school aged students in a format where the pupils are not really involved in the conceptualisation and design of the project. They may be consulted informally perhaps through the process of piloting but that is about the extent of their usual contribution to guiding or owning the research.

With this in mind I thought initially, perhaps naïvely, that it would be interesting and constructive to share our newly published Able Underachiever research findings with a group of secondary aged Able Underachievers and hope that they would want to repeat what we had done to gain specific perspectives on their own school. This was predicated on the notion that if they examined what we had done they would be able to improve on the methodology and ask far better questions based upon their own local school knowledge and interests. I thought this might lead to a real and personal sense of data ownership which would have far greater credibility and consequence than anything that had been brought into their school which was based upon interviews with Able Underachievers who were being educated elsewhere. There is an expression called 'NGIE' which stands for 'No good. Invented elsewhere' which attempts to convey the idea that innovations in schools are far more likely to be accepted if they are developed by local and trusted insiders like students and teachers, rather than by remote and unknown outsiders like researchers.

I also thought this approach would be far more likely to impress the teaching staff and the senior managers so that pupils doing the research might feel the positive effects of their hard work. A desired outcome would be to see some visible evidence that the innovative research of the Able Underachievers was being incorporated into school life and planning and that it was generally valued.

Plan: Proposed Research Project with Able Underachievers September 2002

It is a feature of this Chapter that, rather than providing a critique of the events and practices, the text will provide a journalistic style informed principally by a diary I maintained throughout the project. I invested much in detailed plans of what we could and should do to sell the idea and launch a group of Able Underachievers. With hindsight I am staggered how little of it we needed.

The aim was for the participants to own the project, by leaving the adults to take a secondary role. A major aim was to harness the untapped energy and resources of underachieving able pupils whose contribution to life at school was currently under-utilised. This aim was subsequently met.

If the potential of this group was to be realised we needed to offer something substantial from the start or the energy might dissipate and attendance could deteriorate. I had hoped we could collectively organise a group which would discuss the problems of Able Underachievers, conduct some in-house research with pupils and staff to inform the process and motivate the pupils to propose some innovative and acceptable school-based interventions to address the problems. This was designed to make a noticeable difference to the school.

What actually happened

By September 2002 the staff had nominated five volunteer Able Underachievers to begin the group. All members were pupils who felt themselves to be Able Underachievers and both staff and parents agreed with this description. One new member joined in January 2003. The youngest member was in Year 8 and the oldest was in Year 13. The gender balance was three girls and three boys: the boys were younger than the girls.

The Able Underachiever group at this school was actually launched in October 2002 after a series of meetings with staff. What follows continues the story and shows how widely we moved from original plans. This is not seen as a problem but as a marker of the identity the group created for itself as a highly desirable initial outcome. This story is based upon my memory, diary logs and some tape recordings I kept of earlier meetings of the group.

By Easter 2003 we had met formally on twelve fortnightly Thursday mornings for about one hour in a designated room on the first floor. The work continued after Easter with most of the activity centred upon the Student Teacher Day on 25th June 2003. These words were read by members of the Able Underachiever group and with their help in subsequent revisions this story will hopefully be interpreted as one reasonably accurate reflection of what happened, although from the perspective of myself as an adult, rather than coming directly from the members themselves. They have yet to decide how best to tell their side of the story. One main outcome of the group was a series of demonstrations on a Student Teacher Day organised by the group to show the school community how they themselves would like to be more frequently taught by more active teaching and learning approaches.

This is an account of what was happening within the group.

Session 1

We began on 9th October 2002 with a team building exercise and generally got to know each other. No one felt he or she had been selected for membership by mistake. The pupils had actually been selected by the staff with great imagination and I was instantly struck by the members' intellect, enthusiasm, care, creativity, humour, respect for each other, sharing, co-operation and tolerance for diversity. The project teacher, Tracey, shared these attributes also and the two of us facilitated the Able Underachiever group by adopting a relatively low profile and allowing the members great latitude and freedom in where the work took us. We created a gentle partnership and the group knew that I would be recording the process.

In the first and subsequent meetings we have always had plenty of ideas, some of which have resulted in clearer action than others. We talked about:

- a student newspaper
- recreational development
- coffee bars
- where and when it would be best to meet and for how long
- the ideal group size and composition
- an 'Adult Model' of working together
- others perhaps joining the group later
- avoiding feeling helpless
- staying focused on tasks
- problem identification
- observing underachievement in school
- identifying causes of underachieving
- email communication between meetings
- the school's website, which was organised by a group member
- group cohesion and reflecting on processes occurring within the meeting.

Throughout the life of the group I was impressed by the way the members showed such great respect and support for each other whilst maintaining their own sense of identity. I have seen no signs of competition, rivalry or negativity. Members are very tolerant of each other and under no particular pressure to conform. There has been a pleasing combination of honesty, laughter, volunteering and task completion.

Session 2

By the second meeting on 30th October the group had gelled and got to know each another better. We talked about what had happened at the first meeting. They had not managed to meet independently nor had they formulated an email distribution list for technical reasons. We fixed a regular plan to meet at 9.15 on alternative Thursday mornings.

In the future we hoped to be able to find some protected time to meet which would not mean that members would miss large portions of teaching sessions. We basically needed to find some free time. One solution would be after school or in the evenings or during lunch breaks to remove time pressure but the group felt that using the normal class time gave the project some justifiable status.

We spent some time considering research methods and talked about the use of questionnaires, interviews, observations and focus groups. Members seemed to be familiar with what these methods could offer.

I circulated the group with a list of tentative research questions from my original study to the group for them to address. They volunteered to study these questions with others. Ideally I would have preferred to communicate between meetings via email as this would have thrown up information about the types of discussions students would like to start. Email communication never really materialised because it would have left some members out of the communication loop.

We decided to role play a research type interview. Initials are used to denote group members. K asked J 'How do you think you are doing at school?' The question was ineffective and prompted K to ask 'What are you getting from your lessons?' J's response was 'I am bored.' K's question 'What would make it better?' produced J's response 'Make it more interactive as we write too much in class.' J had picked this idea up himself and wanted to explore it.

This led to a discussion that pupils should share this perspective with teachers. This raised the issue of possibly offending a teacher. K thought we needed to do more preparation if research interviews were to be effective in this school.

Much of the actual session was devoted to a drama exercise designed to follow up comments about some lessons being boring and counter-productive. I wanted to gain a better appreciation of members' insights, creativity, spontaneity and depth of understanding. J volunteered to be the student talking to a teacher about her lessons being a bit boring.

He was quite polite but got the message across to another in role as a receptive classroom teacher. I suggested this simulation after they indicated the impossibility or the sheer difficulty of having this conversation with a teacher. Tracey surprised the group by saying she would really welcome this type of student feedback, if handled properly. This prompted further good communication and some optimism. How could we get teachers to tell pupils that feedback is a good idea? Where is the best setting? Some do not believe feedback would be valued. Could this be part of school culture?

J stressed that there are different ways to learn and that teachers ought to value this. He seemed to be speaking around current research on preferences with learning and teaching styles.

I interrupted the flow at times to get the audience to attend to dynamics and processes, especially the non-verbal ones. I was interested to see what worked and what did not work.

I thought that J did well but another member felt that this was just the 'tip of the iceberg' and that in reality J would actually have a lot more to say if he felt really comfortable. The process introduced the ideas of starting the conversations that need to take place as described in *Listening to Able Underachievers,* along with the notions of learned helplessness and repairing conversations.

Session 3

The third session was on 14th November and by now there was growing interest in doing some research. Simultaneously, the group began to think about some students actually preparing lessons and then teaching these lessons as a way to see if fellow students preferred alternative and more hands-on and practical teaching styles and methods. The group also thought that if some teachers could see first hand evidence of more experiential and interactive teaching taking place, it could perhaps sell them on trying more of it themselves. At this stage the group began to consider a 'Student Teacher Day' as a better approach to research the problems of disinterested students in a more natural way than by using traditional research methods.

On a Student Teacher Day pupils could experiment with teaching, using the methods, styles and techniques which the Able Underachiever group advocated. This might involve more simulations, more interaction and a preferable pupil to teacher talking ratio with the regular adult class teacher witnessing this event. The work could be subsequently evaluated by those being taught and the regular classroom teacher. The group felt that they needed to check this out with friends to see if the plan was both feasible and would result in sufficient volunteer student teachers to make the day successful. The day would definitely have to be seen as a pilot exercise. We also talked about how students could take on other adult roles in schools such as the nurse, caretaker, HT, Deputy HT, librarian, teaching assistants, technicians, secretaries, etc.

Tracey asked what the 'payback' would be for the senior managers and the school if the plan for a Student Teacher Day developed? We agreed that we must demonstrate this first before we could launch a pilot. We would need tight discipline in classes or the regular teacher would have to take over, which would be a lost opportunity and could threaten the long term objectives of this Able Underachiever project. The group agreed that teaching offers a special chance to learn a topic in quite a different way to how we learn as a class.

We agreed on the need to estimate interest in this student teaching proposal. Here the group could make their case by showing staff experientially and dynamically what they mean by what they want to happen in lessons. Videotaping lessons might help but the group thought it would possibly obtrude since watched behaviour is further affected by the use of video cameras.

The group considered that inspirational teaching involves real conversation, more student participation and teachers getting to know pupils as individuals. They valued teachers talking more directly with pupils rather than at pupils and were critical of teachers just handing out information as the dominant way of teaching. They admired teachers who were encouraging pupils to think for themselves. They thought we might need an observational schedule to capture what was being done by pupils in role as teachers.

Session 4

The fourth session was held on 21st November and the group began with a conversation about the use of sets to group pupils. Views on being placed in sets vary. Concern was expressed that sets can disadvantage less able pupils. Atmosphere is thought to be important. Some students were keen to be taught with friends, regardless of their ability. Some students wondered what it would be like to be in a mixed ability class and not feel that their personal needs were addressed. Some work at school was thought to lack challenge and to be boring. Some in the group felt their work did not challenge them.

We shared some feedback on the proposals for student teaching. K and B had found many interested volunteers. Several volunteers wanted to work in pairs to feel safer. Within the Able Underachiever group two members wanted to teach English, a third would teach Drama or Maths or IT. A fourth would teach IT with a partner and a fifth would teach Maths with a partner.

This Student Teacher pilot would generate far more research interest than other methods like questionnaires or interviews or focus groups.

Concern was expressed about how the student teachers would command respect from their students. We would need to address this topic. The problem might be worse with younger student teachers. It was suggested that the volunteers teach pupils younger than themselves so as to minimise the problem of discipline.

We talked about how would we evaluate this student teaching possibly with observation schedules or rating scales. We shared ideas about pupils demonstrating preferred teaching methods to school staff and peers.

One member was very interested in determining preferred learning styles and he thought that by using a questionnaire survey that student teachers would have advanced knowledge of the preferred learning styles of the students facing them in the classrooms. Some work was done on this but it was not completed.

Others thought we still ought to be asking pupils these sorts of questions:

Are you happy with your classes?

What are your interests? (hobbies and clubs)

Do you have any hidden talent?

Is it easy for you to talk with teachers? Tell us more.

How could you improve this school?

There was some debate on how best to seek student opinions. We thought we could get very different responses depending on what the pupils believed we might do with their responses. There might be some fears.

Other research methods we discussed included interviewing teachers, developing the school's website as a place to do research, suggestion boxes and examining student writing.

At one stage we did a free association exercise on the attributes of gifted, talented and inspired teachers. It produced these suggestions:

- having fun and getting involved
- enjoying the subject
- involving you
- showing care about students
- following up your interests
- speaking to you on a first name basis
- talking at your level
- being competent
- setting good expectations and appropriate challenge
- getting respect but not commanding it
- not requesting too much writing
- making a comic or film
- using magic and illusions as a teaching medium.

Session 5

After a long break in the Christmas holidays we met in January and were joined by our newest member A. We agreed meeting times for the term as Thursdays at 9.15-10.15.

There was much serious discussion about future planning and jobs to be done. Reportedly there were lots of volunteers to teach lessons, either alone or in pairs, and more would be welcome. In the time we had together as a planning group we needed to devise a list of tasks to be done and to give deadlines.

Teaching volunteers would need some orientation, help with planning and reassurances about our overall goals and purposes. These volunteers would need to approach given teachers and offer to take over the teaching of designated lessons at certain times. We needed to give volunteers some guidance on how to do this.

Student volunteers would need some protected time with the host teacher to talk about lesson content, teaching materials and resources, delivery style and reassurances about being up to the job so the normal classroom teacher would feel confident about what was to happen. The project team wanted to observe some of these lessons to find out what was actually going on. We needed some time after the event to discuss its outcome and what we want to do next. We thought that a report to the senior management team would be a good idea. If the project was successful there would be further opportunity for students and teachers to work together to plan lessons, look at different teaching styles and consider productive ways to collaborate with one another.

We needed to produce a master planning chart so all the work was scheduled with time slots and named persons carrying out individual responsibilities.

Session 6

We met next on 23rd January and were told that the Student Teacher Day must be seen as relevant and compatible with normal National Curriculum planning. We revisited the whole purpose again and concluded that this day should be really positive and should show staff and pupils how the Able Underachiever group would like to see more lessons planned and executed in the future. Role reversal would be the key feature to show alternative styles of teaching and learning. A high level of respect for student teachers would be achieved through careful planning. The day would be fun, entertaining and inspirational. It would provide work experience for current pupils who were considering a career in teaching. In future it was hoped that some teachers would involve more pupils in lesson planning.

Session 7

We met on 31st January and addressed technical planning issues. Members shared with each other thoughts about what each might teach on the Student Teacher Day whilst reserving time to be available to observe in other lessons taught by pupils and to assist with supervision and management tasks. There was further talk of a questionnaire.

Session 8

We met on 6th February and wrestled again with the learning style preference questionnaire. We wondered if all Year 7 pupils be able to understand it? Was it too long and complicated? What about poor readers? Could we produce two versions? Concern was expressed about how we are spending our time. We hope not to get side-tracked on highly technical issues.

We asked how does knowing a student's preferred learning style help with lesson planning? We tried some demonstrations like the one about wanting to teach swimming where five pupils all have unique learning preferences.

One wants to see swimming visually, by means of videotape, TV, live models, charts, a tour of the swimming pool. One wants to read about the history, philosophy, sociology and psychology of swimming, along with coaching strategies and texts on pool design, swimwear, etc. Another wants to learn experientially and just wants to swim. A fourth wants to just listen to lectures, audio-tapes, etc. A fifth learns best where there is class humour and the integration of several different learning styles.

We agreed that pure knowledge of preferences would not make the student teaching lesson preparation an easy task. It could actually make the lesson preparation more challenging and difficult for beginners. Perhaps all lessons need to have different approaches in evidence and up front.

We then moved on to the purpose and creation of desired learning outcomes or objectives. We thought about warm-ups and closure. We thought about all the anxieties which could surface within lesson planning, much of which centred on the potential for losing control of the pupils. Back up plans were considered highly desirable along with piloting and rehearsals.

The idea of a training session for prospective student teachers to assist with planning and the reduction of anxiety was agreed.

Session 9

We next met on 27th February and determined that 25th June would be the designated Student Teacher Day. The work on the questionnaire on learning styles had not progressed and therefore it was abandoned while we concentrated on recruiting and supporting volunteer student teachers. We focussed on trying to identify the needs, motivation and anxieties of the volunteers. We thought they would need a briefing and spent time planning this.

Assuming the day was successful we hoped to hold a bigger event next year with more student teacher volunteers, more taster sessions over the noon hour and more pupils taking on roles of adults with responsibilities in school. The idea of the 25th June student teacher day being a one-off event would be seen as a setback.

Session 10

Further work was done on planning.

Session 11

We met on 27th March and focused again on the upcoming briefing for volunteers to address their legitimate questions. Two members had briefed the headteacher and reported back his support. We decided that only lessons in Years 7, 8 and 9 would be taught by volunteers from Years 9-13, who would be older and competent to teach the designated subject. Lessons must be carefully organised, with the host teacher who owns the class being covered. Some practical lessons could be problematic.

The briefing would need to address:

- student teacher needs
- aims and objectives for the day
- links to alternative learning styles
- what the organisers are expecting

- working with a partner
- anxieties
- discipline
- general preparation.

Session 12

We met on 10th April and spent time surveying the applications from volunteers. It looked as though we had already recruited about 25 student teachers who would be covering about thirteen lessons on the day. Some had volunteered to teach more than one lesson. These needed to be matched to the overall school timetable for the day. We agreed to accept late volunteering up until the end of April. Four members of the Able Underachiever Group also volunteered to teach and play administrative roles on the day.

Summer Term 2003

We met on 1st, 8th, 22nd May and 11th and 19th June in the final stages of preparation for the Student Teacher Day. The preparations continued with great enthusiasm. Much of the discussion concerned last minute technical details and jobs to be done willingly and responsibly by the Able Underachiever group. About 48 actual pupils volunteered to teach something like 22 lessons, often working in pairs or groups of three. Not every volunteer could be accommodated within the tight time schedule but most were accepted. On 11th June we met with about 40 volunteer students for a final planning session designed to address anxieties and to share with them our expectations and best wishes for the day. It went very well.

On Wednesday 25th June Student Teacher Day materialised. I was fortunate to be able to share in the activity both with the Able Underachiever organisers in their base room and by observing three lessons each taught by a student teacher with two other students assisting in supportive roles. We distributed feedback questionnaires to all the pupils who attended these lessons and gave a separate questionnaire to the host classroom teachers who were there to support the work taking place. Much of what I read and saw was very favourable.

I know the Able Underachievers group will process the written feedback and find a way to report back to the school's senior management team, who supported the project from the beginning. Preliminary analysis of the evaluation survey of pupils showed 223 positive ratings, 71 'okay' ratings and only 30 negative ones. In the three one-hour lessons I observed there was much to process. On the positive side the work was planned, purposeful, disciplined, engaging and effective, given the lack of experience with previous teaching. I witnessed real enthusiasm, the holding of attention and respect, care, creativity and imagination.

I saw clear evidence of spontaneous solutions to unpredictable problems which were dealt with without inducing panic or high levels of anxiety amongst the student teachers. The host teachers could see the value of the exercise and were most helpful to the process. Rewards for success were employed. Noise levels in classrooms appeared to be normal and certainly tolerable. One group went on a successful Biology field trip.

I was however disappointed that some host teachers felt that better and longer planning conversations with the student teachers were needed, that time was lost with registration technicalities and that the actual aims and objectives of some classwork were not adequately covered in the lessons.

One highlight for me was to see an IT lesson taught by a member of the Able Underachiever group and competently backed up by his associates. Despite some technical difficulty accessing the security surrounding the smart white board used for demonstrations, the lesson planning involved opportunities for students to learn a selection of new and relevant IT skills, which they clearly valued. I know this because that is what they told me at the end of this lesson. The work was set so that students could advance at their own rate and learn as much as time allowed. Considerable thought had been invested in a series of handouts and stimulus material which was embedded within the PCs used by the students.

Summary

It was a privilege to participate with this Able Underachiever project from the beginning. The work accomplished reflected very well upon all the participants. We addressed various challenges and overcame them. We learned a great deal from one another. There was much voluntary activity developing in the background which is why I feel the work was so successful. Despite a great deal of laughter and regular bouts of creative spontaneity, we did keep mostly on task and got the essential jobs done. There were many turns in the road and ideas which were not pursued but which is the nature of a highly talented group which is multi-tasking all the time with busy members. Unsurprisingly, I conclude that more student-generated work of this type is needed in schools. At a time when schools are desperate for resources it is a dreadful waste of opportunity not to access more of what students can offer.

This story is still unfinished. We do not know what the Able Under-achiever group will now do with the considerable feedback obtained on the Student Teacher Day.

Bibliography

Achebe, C. (1988 orig. 1959) *Things Fall Apart in The African Trilogy,* London: Picador

American Express Library of Childhood (1993) *Let's Listen to Children: a guide for parents of 0-5 year olds,* Dublin

Ames, C. (1992) Classrooms: goals, structures and student motivation, *Journal of Educational Psychology* 84 261-271

Aries, P. (1962) *Centuries of Childhood,* London: Cape

Armstrong, D. (2003) *Experiences of Special Education: Re-evaluating policy and practice through life stories,* London: RoutledgeFalmer

Armstrong, T. (1995) *The Myth of the ADD Child,* New York: Plume

Askew, M., Brown, M., Rhodes, V., Johnson, D. and William, D. (1997) *Effective Teachers of Numeracy, Final Report for the TTA 1995-6,* London: King's College School of Education

Audit Commission (1994) *Seen But Not Heard: Coordinating Child Health and Social Services for Children in Need,* London: HMSO

Audit Commission (2002) SEN: *A mainstream issue,* London: HMSO.

Barton, L. (1998) Developing an emancipatory research agenda: possibilities and dilemmas in Clough, P. and Barton, L. (eds) *Articulating with Difficulty,* London: Paul Chapman

Barton, L. (1999) Teachers, Change and Professionalism: What's in a name? In L. Barton and F. Armstrong. *Difference and Difficulty: Insights, Issues and Dilemmas,* Sheffield: University of Sheffield Department of Educational Studies

Bell, B. (2002) *Lessons in Lifemanship,* (Online Book) http://bbll.com/#Top

Bene E. and Anthony J. (1978) *Family Relations Test (revised),* Windsor: NFER-Nelson

Bennathan, M. and Boxall, M. (1996) *Effective Intervention in Primary Schools: Nurture Groups,* London: David Fulton

Biehal, N., Clayden, J., Stein, M., and Wade, J. (1995) *Moving on: Young People and Leaving Care Schemes,* London: HMSO

Billington, T. (1995) Acknowledging interpretation in everyday practice: a discourse analytic approach, *Educational Psychology in Practice*, 50, 17-26

Billington, T. (2000) *Separating, Losing and Excluding Children: Narratives of Difference*, London: Routledge Falmer

Billington, T. (2002) Children, Psychologists and Knowledge, a discourse-analytic narrative in Educational and Child Psychology, *British Psychological Society,* 19, 3, 32-41

Billington, T. (2003) Discourses on Mind: feeling, thinking and learning, Keynote address to the Annual Conference of the Division of Educational and Child Psychology, Harrogate, January, British Psychological Society

Billington, T. and Warner, S. (2003) Editorial in *Educational and Child Psychology* 20 (1) 4-6

Billington, T. and Warner, S. (eds. 2003) Child Protection: critical theory, research and practice, *Educational and Child Psychology,* 20 (1) Leicester: British Psychological Society

Bion, W.R. (1970) *Attention and interpretation: A scientific approach to insight in psychoanalysis and groups,* London: Tavistock Publications

Bourdieu, P. (1984) *Distinction: A social critique of the judgment of taste,* London: Routledge and Kegan Paul

Boxall, M. (2002) *Nurture Groups in School,* London: Paul Chapman

British Psychological Society (1996) *Attention Deficit Hyperactivity Disorder AD/HD, A psychological response to an evolving concept,* Leicester: British Psychological Society

Brodie, I. (2000) Children's Homes and School Exclusion: Redefining the problem in *Support for Learning,* 15 (1), February, 2000 25 – 29

Burden, R. (1997) in Lindsay, G. and Thompson, D. *Values into Practice in Special Education,* London: David Fulton

Burman, E. (1994) *Deconstructing Developmental Psychology*, London: Routledge

Burman, E., Aitken, G., Alldred, P., Allwood, R., Billington, T., Goldberg, B., Gordo Lopez, A., Heenan, C., Marks, D. and Warner, S. (1996) *Psychology, Discourse Practice: from Regulation to Resistance,* London: Taylor and Francis

Butroyd, R. (2001) National Curriculum Subjects are Repositories of Values that are Under-Explored in Cullingford, C. and Oliver, P. (2001) *The National Curriculum and its effects*, Aldershot: Ashgate

Celltech (2001) *Be Cool!* Slough Berkshire: Celltech Pharmaceuticals Ltd.

Children Act, The (1989) London: HMSO

Clough, P. (1998) Differently articulate? Some indices of disturbed/disturbing voices in Clough, P. and Barton, L. (eds) *Articulating with Difficulty*, London: Paul Chapman

Clough, P. and Barton, L. (eds. 1998) *Articulating with Difficulty: Research Voices in Inclusive Education,* London: Sage/Paul Chapman Publications

Cooper, P. (2002) *The Effectiveness of Nurture Groups: Findings from Research and Evaluation,* Midlands Nurture Group Network, May

Cooper, P. and Shea, T. (1998) Pupils' perceptions of AD/HD, *Emotional and Behavioural Difficulties*, 3(3), 36-45

Cooper, P. Arnold, R. and Boyd, E. (2001) The Effectiveness of Nurture Groups: Preliminary Research Findings *British Journal of Special Education*, 28, (4) 160-166

Cooper, P., Arnold, R. and Boyd, E. (1999) *The Nature and Distribution of Nurture Groups in England and Wales*, Cambridge: Cambridge University School of Education

Corbett, J. (1998) 'Voice' in emancipatory research: imaginative listening in Clough, P. and Barton, L. (eds) *Articulating with Difficulty,* London: Paul Chapman

Coulling, N. (2000) Definitions of successful education for the 'looked after' child: A multi-agency perspective in *Support for Learning* 15(1) 30-35

Department for Education (1994) *Code of Practice on the Identification and Assessment of Special Educational Needs*, London: HMSO

Department for Education and Department of Health (2000) *Education of Young People in Public Care (Guidance)* London: DfEE/DoH

Department for Education and Employment (1997) *Excellence for All Children: Meeting Special Educational Needs*, London: DfEE

Department for Education and Employment (1998) *Meeting Special Educational Needs: A programme of action*, Suffolk: DfEE

Department for Education and Employment (1998) *The National Literacy Strategy: a framework for teaching,* London: DfEE

Department for Education and Employment (1999) *Social Inclusion and Pupil Support, Circular,* 10/99

Department for Education and Employment (2000) *Educational Psychology Services (England) Current Role, Good Practice and Future Directions. Report of the Working Group*, London: DfEE

Department for Education and Employment (2001) *Promoting Children's Mental Health within Early Years and School Settings,* London: DfEE

Department of Education and Science, *Education Act 1981*, London: HMSO

Department of Education and Science (1989) *English for ages 5 to 16 (The Cox Report)*, London: HMSO

Department for Education and Skills (2001) *Learning to Listen; Core Principles for the Involvement of Children and Young People*, Nottingham: DfES

Department for Education and Skills (2001) *Special Educational Needs Code of Practice,* Nottingham: DfES Publications

Department for Education and Skills (2001) *Special Educational Needs and Disability Rights Act*, Nottingham: DfES

Department for Education and Skills (2002) *Special Educational Needs Code of Practice, revised*, Nottingham: DfES Publications

Department for Education and Skills (2003) *The Green Paper: Every Child Matters,* Norwich: The Stationery Office

Department of Health (1998) *The Quality Protects Programme: Transforming Children's Services*, London: Department of Health

Department of Health (2001) *Children's Taskforce: Principles for the Participation of Children, Young People and Families in the Children's Taskforce*, London: Department of Health

Department of Health (2001) *Consent – what you have a right to expect. A guide for children and young people*, Department of Health Publications

Department of Health, Department for Education and Employment and the Home Office (2000) *Framework for Assessment of Children in Need and their families*, London: The Stationery Office

Derrida (1992) in Biesta, G.J.J. Preparing for the Incalculable in Biesta, G.J.J. and Egea-Kuehne, D. (2001), *Derrida and Education*, London: Routledge

Dickens, C. (ed. Paul Schlicke, 1989) *Hard Times*, Oxford: Oxford University Press

Doyle, R. (2002) Using a Readiness scale for reintegrating pupils with social, emotional and behavioural difficulties from a Nurture Group into a mainstream classroom, *British Journal of Special Education*, 29, (2) 126-132

Farrell, P. Ainscow, M., Howes, A., Frankham, J., Fox, S. and Davis, P. (2004 in press)

First Key (1999) *Education 'Looked After': a training pack for teachers*, Leeds: First Key

Foucault, M. (1977) *Discipline and Punish: the Birth of the Prison*, London: Allen Lane

Foucault, M (1982) 'The subject and power': An afterword, in Dreyfus, J. and Rabinow, P. *Michel Foucault: Beyond Structuralism and Hermeneutics,* Chicago Il: University of Chicago Press

Fulcher, G. (1999) *Disabling policies? A comparative approach to education policy and disability*, Sheffield: Falmer Press

Gamman, R. (2002) English is more than just literacy, Ed D thesis: University of Sheffield

Gold, K (2003) What a disaster we created (Interview with Mary Warnock), London *Times Educational Supplement,* 19th September 2003

Goldstein, S. and Goldstein, M. (1998) *Understanding and managing attention disorders in children, a guide form practitioners* (2nd edition), New York: Wiley

Goodman, R. (1997) The Strengths and Difficulties Questionnaire: A research note *Journal of Child Psychology and Psychiatry*, 38, 581-586

Goodwyn, A. and Findlay, K. (1999) The Cox models revisited: English teachers' views of their subject and the National Curriculum in *English in Education*, 33, 2, 19-31

Gould, S. J. (1981) *The Mismeasure of Man,* London: Penguin Books

Harre, R. (1986) *The Social Construction of Emotion,* Oxford: Blackwell

Hayward, P. and Bright, J. (1997) Stigma and mental illness. A review and critique in *Journal of Mental Health*, 6 (4), 345-354

Health Development Agency (2000) *National Healthy School Standard,* Nottingham: DfES DoH

Herts, B. (2001) *Children's Task Force*, London: Department of Health

Hollway, W. (1989) *Subjectivity and Method in Psychology,* London: Sage

Hollway, W. and Jefferson, T. (2000) *Doing Qualitative Research Differently: Free Association, Narrative and the Interview Method*, London: Sage

Hutchby, I. and Moran-Ellis, J. (eds) (1998) *Children and social competence: Arenas of action*, London: Falmer

Inclusive Education for all: Dream or reality, *The Journal of International Special Needs Education*

Inter-agency Cooperation in *Children and Society*, 15 315-332

Irish Society for the Prevention of Cruelty to Children (1996) The Inclusion International, in Reiser, R. and Peasley, H. (2002) *Disability, Equality in Education: Inclusion in Schools Course Book*, London: Disability, Equality and Education

James, A., Jenks, C. and Prout, A. (1998) *Theorizing Childhood*, Oxford: Blackwell

James, S. (2000) A case study of the possible key variables related to self-handicapping strategies used by ten-year-old pupils, Unpublished doctoral thesis, The University of Sheffield

Joseph Rowntree Foundation (1999) *Supporting Disabled Children and their Families, Foundations research summary*, York: Joseph Rowntree Foundation

Kahn, J. and Russell, P (1999) *Quality Protects: First analysis of management action plans with reference to disabled children and their families*, London: Council for Disabled Children

Kelly, G. (1955) *The Psychology of Personal Construct*, New York: Norton

Kewley, G. (1999) The role of medication in a multi-modal approach to the management of ADHD in P. Cooper and K. Bilton (eds) *ADHD, Research, Practice and Opinion*, London: Whurr Publishers

Kierkegaard (1842) in MacIntyre, A. (1985), *After Virtue* (2nd ed.) London: Duckworth Publishers

Klein, M. (1988 orig. 1952) *The Origins of Transference in Envy and Gratitude and Other Works 1946-63*, London: Virago

Klein, M. (1988 orig. 1957) *Envy and Gratitude in Envy and Gratitude and Other Works 1946-63*, London: Virago

Kuehne, D. (2001) *Derrida and Education*, London: Routledge

Lacan, J. (1977) *Ecrits*, London: Routledge

Laing, R.D. (1961) *Self and Others*, London: Pelican

Law, J., Lindsay, G., Peacey, N., Gascoigne, M., Soloff, N., Radford, J. and Band, S. (2001) Facilitating communication between education and health services: the provision for children with speech and language needs in *British Journal of Special Education* 28(3) 133-137

Lee, N. (2003) Child Protection and ambiguity, *Educational and Child Psychology*, 10 (1) 43-52, British Psychological Society.

Lefebvre, H. (1975) in Soja, E.W. (1996) *Thirdspace*, Oxford: Blackwell

Lloyd Bennett, P. and Billington, T. (eds. 2001) Multidisciplinary Work for Children with Autism, *Educational and Child Psychology*, 18 (2) Leicester: British Psychological Society

Lloyd-Smith, M. and Tarr, J. (2000) Researching children's perspectives: a sociological dimension in Lewis, A. and Lindsay, G. (eds) (2000) *Researching children's perspectives*, Buckingham: Open University Press

Lord Laming (2003) *Victoria Climbie Inquiry*, the Summary report of an inquiry, Norwich: HMSO

MacIntyre, A. (1985) *After virtue* (2nd ed.) London: Duckworth Publishers

Maras, P., Cooper, P. and Norwich, B (2002) Hyperactive EBD *Special Children* Summer, 28-31

Maras, P., Redmayne, T., Hall, C., Braithwaite, D., and Prior, P. (1997) Helicopter children and butterfly brains: ADHD perceptions, issues and implications in *Educational and Child Psychology*, 14 (1) 39-49

Marchant, R. and Gordon, R. (2001) *Two-Way Street: Communicating with Disabled Children and Young People,* Dublin: NSPCC, Joseph Rowntree Foundation and Triangle

Markham, E. (1936) *Outwitted* in Felleman, H. (Ed) *The Best Loved Poems of the American People,* Doubleday, 1936, 67

Maslow A H (1954) *Motivation and Personality,* New York: Harper and Row

Mental Health Foundation (1999) *Bright Futures*, London: Mental Health Foundation

Merritt, J. (1995) Attention Deficit Disorder – A Dubious Diagnosis? Television Documentary, Public Broadcasting Service. October 20th

Miller, E.J. (Ed) (1976) *Task and Organisation*, London: Wiley and Sons

Miller, E.J. and Rice, A.K. (1967) *Systems of Organisation*, London: Tavistock Publications

Moore, M. (ed. 2000) *Insider Perspectives on Inclusion: raising voices, raising issues*, Sheffield: Philip Armstrong Publications

Morgan, D.L. (1997) *Focus Groups as Qualitative Research* (2nd edition), London: Sage

Morris, J. (2001) Preface in Marchant, R. and Gordon, R. (2001) *Two-Way Street: Communicating with Disabled Children and Young People,* Dublin: NSPCC, Joseph Rowntree Foundation and Triangle

Mosley, J. (1996) *Quality Circle Time in the Primary Classroom,* Wisbech: LDA

Murray, P. and Penman, J. (2000) *Telling Our Own Stories; reflections on family life in a disabling world,* Sheffield: Parents with Attitude

Network 81, 1-7 Woodfield Terrace, Stansted, Essex, CM24 8AJ

Newton, C., Taylor, J., Wilson, D., (1996) Circles of friends. An inclusive approach to meeting emotional and behavioural needs in *Educational Psychology in Practice* 11(4), 41-48

Nixon, J. (2001), Imagining ourselves into being: Conversing with Hannah Arendt, in *Pedagogy, Culture and Society*, 9 (2), 221-236

Normington, J. and Kyriacou, C. (1994) Exclusion from high schools and the work of the outside agencies involved in *Pastoral Care*, 12(4) 12-15

NSW Commission for Children and Young People (2001) Ask the Children. Prescription and over the counter medication: research into the views and experiences of children and young people in New South Wales in NSW Commission for Children and Young People, www.kids.nsw.gov.au/ask/longversion.html

O'Regan, F. (2002) *How to Teach and Manage children with ADHD*, Wisbech, Cambridgeshire: LDA

Ofsted (2000) *Evaluating Educational Inclusion: Guidance for inspectors and school*, London: Office for Standards in Education

Ofsted (2003) *Handbook for Inspecting Secondary Schools,* Ofsted Publications, London: HMSO

BIBLIOGRAPHY

Oliver, P. (2001) Conceptual issues in a centralised curriculum in Cullingford, C. and Oliver, P. (2001) *The National Curriculum and its effects,* Aldershot: Ashgate

Pomerantz M. and Pomerantz, K.A. (2002) *Listening to Able Underachievers: Creating Opportunities for Change,* London: David Fulton

Prosser, B. (1999) Behaviour Management or Management Behaviour: a sociological analysis of Attention Deficit Hyperactivity Disorder in Australian and American schools, unpublished thesis, Adelaide, Australia: Flinders University

Prosser, B. (2004) *People, Politics and a Pill: ADHD and adolescents in Australia.* Australia: Pluto Press, in press

Qualifications and Curriculum Authority (1998) *Education for Citizenship and the Teaching of Democracy in Schools,* London: QCA

Rapport, M.D., and Kelly, K.L. (1991) Psychostimulant effects on learning and cognitive function, findings and implications for children with attention deficit hyperactivity disorder in *Clinical Psychology Review,* 11, 61-92

Reynolds, D., Hopkins, D., Potter, D., Chapman, C. (2001) School Improvement for Schools Facing Challenging Circumstances: A Review of research and Practice, Unpublished report from Schools of Education at Nottingham and Exeter Universities

Rieser, R. and Mason, M. (1990) *Disability Equality in the Classroom: A Human Rights Issue,* London: Disability Equality in Education

Rieser, R. and Peasley, H. (2002) *Disability, Equality in Education: Inclusion in Schools Course Book,* London: Disability, Equality and Education

Robson, C. (2002) *Real World Research* (2nd edition) Oxford: Blackwell

Rogers, C. (1951) *Client-Centered Therapy,* Constable and Company: London

Root, R. and Reswick, R. (2003) An update on the diagnosis and treatment of attention-deficit/hyperactivity disorder in children, *Professional Psychology: Research and Practice,* 34 (1), 34-41

Rose, N. (1989) *Governing the Soul,* London: Routledge

Ruddock, J., Chaplain, R., Wallace, G. (1996) *School Improvement: What Can Pupils Tell Us?* London: David Fulton

Sammons, P., Hillman, J. and Mortimore, P. (1995) *Key Characteristics of Effective Schools,* London: HMSO

Social Exclusion Unit (1998) *Truancy and School Exclusion,* London: The Stationery Office

Social Exclusion Unit (1999) *Bridging the Gap: New Opportunities for 16-18 Year Olds Not in Education, Employment or Training,* London: The Stationery Office

Social Services Inspectorate and Office for Standards in Education (1995) *The Education of Children who are Looked After by Local Authorities,* London: Crown Copyright

Soja, E.W. (1996), *Thirdspace,* Oxford: Blackwell

Steiner, C. (1984) Emotional Literacy, *Transactional Analysis Journal,* 14, 162-173

Stevens, D. (1998) Finding the Perfect Balance in *English in Education,* 32, 1, 38-44

Tannock, R. (1998) Attention Deficit Hyperactivity Disorder. Advances in Cognitive, Neurobiological and Genetic Research, *Journal of Child Psychology and Psychiatry* 39(1), 65-99

179

Times Educational Supplement October 6, 2000

UNESCO (1994) *The Salamanca Statement and Framework for Action on Special Needs Education,* Paris: UNESCO

Unicef (1989) *UN Convention on the Rights of the Child*, Office of the High Commissioner for Human Rights, Geneva: Switzerland

Utting Report (1991) *Children in the Public Care*, London: HMSO

Volkow, N. (2001) Therapeutic Doses or Oral Methylphenidate Significantly Increase Extracellular Dopamine in the Human Brain, *Journal of Neuroscience* 21 (2)

Warnock, M. (1978) *Special Educational Needs: report of the committee of enquiry into the education of handicapped children and young people*, London: HMSO

Webb, R. and Vulliamy, G. (2001) Joining up Solutions: the Rhetoric and Practice of Inter-agency Cooperation in *Children and Society*, 15 315-332

Weithorn, C.J., (1979) Perspectives on drug treatment for hyperactivity in M. J. Cohen *Drugs and Special Children*, New York: Gardner Press

Weston, N. and Williams, T. (2000) *Health for Life*, Cheltenham: Nelson Thornes

White, M. and Epston, D. (1990) *Narrative Means to Therapeutic Ends*, London: W.W. Norton and Company Ltd

Willig, C. (2001) *Introducing Qualitative Research in Psychology: Adventures in theory and method,* London: Open University Press

Willis, B. (1994) Behaviour Policy and Staff, Support: Helping Schools to Help Themselves' *Educational Psychology in Practice*, 10 (3) 150 – 154

Zametkin, A.J. and Ernst, M. (1999) Problems in the management of Attention-Deficit Hyperactivity Disorder in *New England Journal of Medicine* 340(1), 40-46

Index